knitted wild animals

knitted wild animals

15 adorable, easy-to-knit toys

Sarah Keen

Watson-Guptill Publications/New York

Copyright © 2009 by GMC Publications Ltd
Text copyright © 2009 by Sarah Keen

Published in the United States by Watson-Guptill
Publications, an imprint of the Crown Publishing
Group, a division of Random House, Inc.,
New York.
www.crownpublishing.com
www.watsonguptill.com

WATSON-GUPTILL is a registered trademark and
the WG and Horse designs are trademarks of
Random House, Inc.

Originally published in Great Britain by
Guild of Master Craftsman Publications Ltd,
Lewes, East Sussex, in 2009.

Library of Congress Control Number
2010924468

ISBN 978-0-8230-3318-8

Printed in China

Design by Rebecca Mothersole

Illustrations by Simon Rodway, except
for those on page 114 and at the right
of page 122, which are copyright © 2009
by Sarah Keen

10 9 8 7 6 5 4 3 2 1

First American Edition

I would like to thank the following people for their kindness and support:

Cynthia, Dr Ruth and Dr Nicholls;

Cheryl, Liz and Eirwen;

Maureen, Mary and Shirley.

Special thanks to my parents.

Special thanks also to Clare Wools, Aberystwyth, Wales,

and to Jonathan Bailey and all the team at GMC Publications.

Where those wild animals hide

The animals

Techniques

Introduction

I learned to knit as a child and have made numerous soft toys,
baby clothes and garments. I found calculating stitches fascinating
and soon was writing my own knitting patterns from scratch. I've
experimented with different arts and crafts but knitting, for me,
is what I want to do most of all.

This book started with the monkey and elephant and then grew
to be a book of 15 different wild animals. Hopefully there's
something in it that's appealing to everyone. I have enjoyed
creating these animals and hope you too will find enjoyment in
whichever pattern you decide to knit.

GIRAFFE >> 46

ZEBRA >> 52

LION >> 56

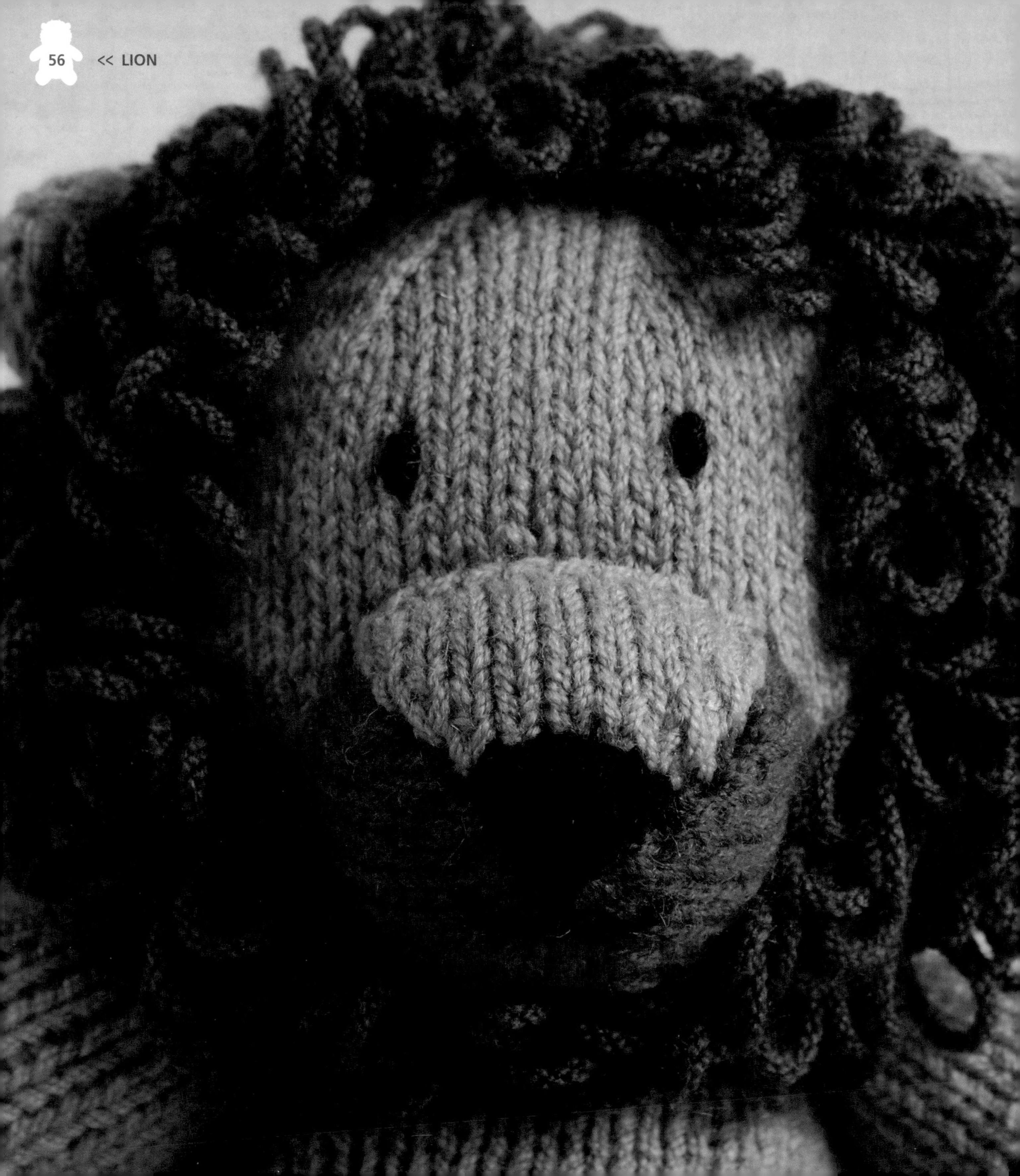

66 << TIGER

HIPPO >> 86

WARTHOG >> 94

A moose with many friends

Busy lions

Snakes you can trust

Absent-minded elephants

Just plain sensible monkeys

The animals

Elephants take dust or mud baths to clean themselves and to protect their skin from the sun, wind, and insects. Their skin is so sensitive that they can even feel a fly landing on it! Elephants love playing in water and drink around 30 gallons of it every day.

ELEPHANT

What you'll need

Measurement
Elephant measures 9½in (24cm) in height

Materials
Any light worsted weight yarn:
350yd (1¾oz/100g) gray (A)
70yd (¾oz/20g) white (B)
Scraps of black for features
*Note: amounts are generous
but approximate*
A pair of size 3 U.S. (3.25mm) needles
Polyester fiberfill
Straight pins
Tweezers for stuffing small parts (optional)

Gauge
26 sts x 34 rows measure 4in (10cm) square
over Stockinette st using 3.25mm needles
before stuffing

Abbreviations
See page 124

How to make Elephant

Body (make 2 pieces)
Beg at lower edge using the thumb method and A, cast on 35 sts.
First and next 4 foll alt rows: P.
Inc row: K10, m1, k15, m1, k10 (37 sts).
Inc row: K11, m1, k15, m1, k11 (39 sts).
Inc row: K12, m1, k15, m1, k12 (41 sts).
Inc row: K13, m1, k15, m1, k13 (43 sts).
Inc row: K14, m1, k15, m1, k14 (45 sts).
Beg with a p row, work in St st for 11 rows.
Dec row: K2tog, k to last 2 sts, k2tog tbl.
Next row: P.
Rep last 2 rows 12 more times (19 sts).
Bind off.

Base
Using the thumb method and A, cast on 20 sts.
First row: P.
Inc row: K1, m1, k to last st, m1, k1.
Rep first 2 rows 5 more times (32 sts).
Beg with a p row, work in St st for 5 rows.
Dec row: K2tog, k to last 2 sts, k2tog tbl.
Next row: P.
Rep last 2 rows 5 more times (20 sts).
Bind off.

Hind legs (make 2)
Using the thumb method and A, cast on 32 sts.
Beg with a p row, work in St st for 21 rows.
Dec row: (K2, k2tog) to end (24 sts).
Next and next foll alt row: P
Dec row: (K1, k2tog) to end (16 sts).
Dec row: (K2tog) to end (8 sts).
Thread yarn through rem sts, pull tight and secure.

Forelegs (make 2)
Using the thumb method and A, cast on 28 sts.
Beg with a p row, work in St st for 15 rows.
Dec row: (k2tog) 3 times, k2, (k2tog) 6 times, k2, (k2tog) 3 times (16 sts).
P 1 row.
Bind off.

Head
Beg at back using the thumb method and A, cast on 12 sts.
First and next 8 foll alt rows: P.
Inc row: (Inc) to end (24 sts).
Inc row: (K3, inc) to end (30 sts).
Inc row: (K4, inc) to end (36 sts).
Inc row: (K5, inc) to end (42 sts).
Inc row: (K6, inc) to end (48 sts).
Inc row: (K7, inc) to end (54 sts).
Inc row: (K8, inc) to end (60 sts).
Inc row: (K9, inc) to end (66 sts).
Inc row: (K10, inc) to end (72 sts).
Beg with a p row, work in St st for 15 rows.
Dec row: (K7, k2tog) to end (64 sts).
Next row: P50, turn.
Next row: S1k, k35, turn.
Next row: S1p, p to end.
Dec row: (K6, k2tog) to end (56 sts).
Next row: P44, turn.
Next row: S1k, k31, turn.
Next row: S1p, p to end.
Dec row: (K5, k2tog) to end (48 sts).
Next row: P38, turn.
Next row: S1k, k27, turn.
Next row: S1p, p to end.
Dec row: (K4, k2tog) to end (40 sts).
Next row: P32, turn.
Next row: S1k, k23, turn.
Next row: S1p, p to end.
Dec row: (K3, k2tog) to end (32 sts).
Next row: P.

Next 2 rows: K.
Dec row: K2tog, k to last 2 sts, k2tog tbl.
Rep last 4 rows 4 more times (22 sts).
Next row: P.
Next 3 rows: K.
Rep last 4 rows 8 more times.
P 1 row.
Dec row: K2, (k2tog) 4 times, k2, (k2tog) 4 times, k2 (14 sts).
Cast off p-wise.

Ears
Side 1 (make 2 pieces)
Using the thumb method and A, cast on 16 sts.
First and next 10 foll alt rows: P.
Inc row: K1, m1, k8, m1, k6, m1, k1 (19 sts).
Inc row: K10, m1, k9 (20 sts).
Inc row: K10, m1, k10 (21 sts).
Inc row: K10, m1, k11 (22 sts).
Inc row: K10, m1, k12 (23 sts).
Inc row: K10, m1, k13 (24 sts).
Inc row: K10, m1, k14 (25 sts).
Inc row: K10, m1, k15 (26 sts).
Shape next row: K2tog, k8, m1, k14, k2tog tbl (25 sts).
Shape next row: K2tog, k7, m1, k14, k2tog tbl (24 sts).
Shape next row: K2tog, k6, m1, k14, k2tog tbl (23 sts).
Dec row: P2tog tbl, p to last 2 sts, p2tog (21 sts).
Bind off.
Side 2 (make 2 pieces)
Using the thumb method and A, cast on 16 sts.
First and next 10 foll alt rows: P.
Inc row: K1, m1, k6, m1, k8, m1 k1 (19 sts).

Inc row: K9, m1, k10 (20 sts).
Inc row: K10, m1, k10 (21 sts).
Inc row: K11, m1, k10 (22 sts).
Inc row: K12, m1, k10 (23 sts).
Inc row: K13, m1, k10 (24 sts).
Inc row: K14, m1, k10 (25 sts).
Inc row: K15, m1, k10 (26 sts).
Shape next row: K2tog, k14, m1, k8, k2tog tbl (25 sts).
Shape next row: K2tog, k14, m1, k7, k2tog tbl (24 sts).
Shape next row: K2tog, k14, m1, k6, k2tog tbl (23 sts).
Dec row: P2tog tbl, p to last 2 sts, p2tog (21 sts).
Bind off.

Tusks (make 2)
Using the thumb method and B, cast on 4 sts.
Inc row: P this row increasing p-wise into first and last st.
Inc row: K this row increasing k-wise into first and last st.
Rep last 2 rows once (12 sts).
Beg with a p row, work in St st for 16 rows decreasing one st at each end of 4th and every foll 4th row (4 sts).
P 1 row.
Thread yarn through sts, pull tight and secure.

Assembly
Body
Place two halves of body together, matching all edges and join row-ends. Stuff body, leaving neck and lower edge open.

Base
Pin base to lower edge of body and sew base to body all the way around, adding more stuffing to base if needed.

Hind legs
Join row-ends of hind legs and stuff. Stand body on flat surface and position legs wide apart, pin and sew cast-on sts of legs to body all the way around.

Forelegs
Fold bound-off sts in half and whipstitch. Join row-ends and stuff. Pin each foreleg to either side of body pinning top of arm to 6th row below bound-off sts at neck. Sew cast-on sts in place all the way around.

Head
Gather cast-on sts of head, pull tight and secure. Join row-ends of trunk and with seam at center back, whipstitch bound-off sts. Stuff trunk and join row-ends of head leaving a gap. Stuff head and close gap. Pin head to body, pinning first garter st row of trunk to neck at center front, adding more stuffing to neck if needed. Sew head to body by taking a small horizontal st from head and then a small horizontal st from body, alternating all the way around.

Ears
With right sides facing, place a side 1 and side 2 together matching all edges. Join row-ends and bound-off sts by sewing back and forth 1 st in from edge. Turn right-side out and catch cast-on sts together. Repeat for the other ear. Sew ears to head.

Tusks
Join row-ends of tusks from tips to beg of increase sts, and stuff, pushing stuffing in with tweezers or tip of scissors. Sew tusks to either side of head at top of trunk.

Embroidering the features
To make eyes, tie a knot in 2 lengths of black yarn, winding the yarn around 6 times to make each knot (see page 122). Check that the knots are the same size. Tie eyes to 15th row above top of trunk with 8 knitted sts in between. Weave in ends into head.

Tail
Take 6 lengths of yarn, each 16in (40cm) long, in a bundle and tie a knot in the center. Fold in half and divide into 3. Braid for 1¼in (3cm) and tie a knot to secure. Cut ends ⅝in (1.5cm) from the knot. Sew tail to elephant at back.

The giraffe is the world's tallest animal and can grow up to 18 feet high with feet the size of dinner plates. They sleep standing up for just 10 minutes to 2 hours each day! Newborn giraffe calves begin their lives by falling 6 feet to the ground, head first. . . . Ouch!

GIRAFFE

DID YOU KNOW?
The mighty giraffe can drink 12 gallons in one sitting . . . . Thirsty giraffe!

What you'll need

Measurement
Giraffe measures 10in (26cm) in height

Materials
Any light worsted weight yarn:
175yd (1¾oz/50g) brown (A)
175yd (1¾oz/50g) yellow (B)
88yd (1oz/25g) cream (C)
Scrap of black for features
Note: amounts are generous but approximate
A pair of size 3 U.S. (3.25mm) needles
Polyester fiberfill
Straight pins

Gauge
26 sts x 34 rows measure 4in (10cm) square over Stockinette st using 3.25mm needles before stuffing

Pattern notes
Before beginning to knit, wind yarns A and B into two separate balls

Abbreviations
See page 124

Our giraffe asks whether sleeping standing up is really such a good idea.

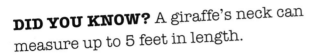

DID YOU KNOW? A giraffe's neck can measure up to 5 feet in length.

How to make Giraffe
Body (make 2 pieces)
Note: Two separate balls of A and B are required.

Beg at the lower edge. Using the thumb method and one strand of A, cast on 35 sts.

First and next foll 4 alt rows: P.

Inc row: K10, m1, k15, m1, k10 (37 sts).
Inc row: K11, m1, k15, m1, k11 (39 sts).
Inc row: K12, m1, k15, m1, k12 (41 sts).
Inc row: K13, m1, k15, m1, k13 (43 sts).
Inc row: K14, m1, k15, m1, k14 (45 sts).
Next row: P.

Join in B and second ball of A and work in blocks of color, using a separate ball for each block and twisting when changing yarn.

Pattern
Row 1: K, using B.
Row 2: P2-A (second ball), p41-B, p2-A (first ball).
Row 3: K4-A, k37-B, k4-A.
Row 4: P5-A, p35-B, p5-A.
Row 5: K2tog, k5-A, k31-B, k5, k2tog tbl-A (43 sts).
Row 6: P7-A, p29-B, p7-A.

Row 7: K2tog, k7-A, k25-B, k7, k2tog tbl-A (41 sts).
Row 8: P9-A, p23-B, p9-A.
Row 9: K2tog, k9-A, k19-B, k9, k2tog tbl-A (39 sts).
Row 10: P11-A, p17-B, p11-A.
Row 11: K2tog, k11-A, k13-B, k11, k2tog tbl-A (37 sts).
Row 12: P13-A, p11-B, p13-A.
Row 13: K2tog, k13-A, k7-B, k13, k2tog tbl-A (35 sts).
Row 14: P15-A, p5-B, p15-A.
Row 15: K2tog, k15-A, k1-B, k15, k2tog tbl-A (33 sts).

Row 16: P-A (second ball).
Row 17: K2tog, k13-A, k3-B, k13, k2tog tbl-A (31 sts).
Row 18: P13-A, p5-B, p13-A.
Row 19: K2tog, k10-A, k7-B, k10, k2tog tbl-A (29 sts).
Row 20: P10-A, p9-B, p10-A.
Row 21: K2tog, k7-A, k11-B, k7, k2tog tbl-A (27 sts).
Row 22: P7-A, p13-B, p7-A.
Row 23: K2tog, k4-A, k15-B, k4, k2tog tbl-A (25 sts).
Row 24: P4-A, p17-B, p4-A.
Row 25: K2tog, k1-A, k19-B, k1, k2tog tbl-A (23 sts).
Break off A and cont in B.
Rows 26, 28, 30 and 32: P.
Rows 27, 29, 31 and 33: K2tog, k to last 2 sts, k2tog tbl.
15 sts now rem with WS facing for next row.
Change to A.
Row 34: P-A.
Row 35: K2tog, k to last 2 sts, k2tog tbl-A (13 sts).
Rows 36 and 38: P-A.
Rows 37 and 39: K-A.
Join in 2 balls of B.
Row 40: P2-B, p9-A, p2-B (second ball).
Row 41: K3-B, k7-A, k3-B.
Row 42: P4-B, p5-A, p4-B.
Row 43: K5-B, k3-A, k5-B.
Row 44: P6-B, p1-A, p6-B.
Row 45: K-B (first ball)
Row 46: P6-B, p1-A, p6-B.
Row 47: K5-B, k3-A, k5-B.
Row 48: P4-B, p5-A, p4-B.
Row 49: K3-B, k7-A, k3-B.
Row 50: P2-B, p9-A, p2-B.
Cont in A, work in St st for 6 rows.
Bind off.

Base
Using the thumb method and A, cast on 20 sts.
First row: P.
Inc row: K1, m1, k to last st, m1, k1.
Rep these 2 rows 5 times more (32 sts).
Beg with a p row, work in St st for 5 rows.
Dec row: K2tog, k to last 2 sts, k2tog tbl.
Next row: P.
Rep last 2 rows 5 times more (20 sts).
Bind off.

Hind legs (make 2)
Beg at hoof using the thumb method and C, cast on 6 sts.
P 1 row.
Inc row: (Inc) to end.
Rep last 2 rows once (24 sts).
P 1 row.
Work 2 rows in garter st.
Beg with a k row, work in St st for 2 rows.
Dec row: (K1, k2tog) to end (16 sts).
Beg with a p row, work in St st for 5 rows.
Change to A.
Dec row: (K2tog) to end (8 sts).
P 1 row.
Inc row: K1, (m1, k1) to end (15 sts).
P 1 row.
Inc row: (K1, m1, k1, m1, k1) to end (25 sts).
Beg with a p row, work in St st for 11 rows.
Change to B and work in St st for 10 rows.
Dec row: K1, (k2tog, k1) to end (17 sts).
P 1 row.
Bind off.

Forelegs (make 2)
Beg at hoof using the thumb method and C, cast on 6 sts.
P 1 row.
Inc row: (Inc) to end.
Rep last 2 rows once (24 sts).
P 1 row.
Garter st 2 rows.

Beg with a k row, work in St st for 2 rows.
Dec row: (K1, k2tog) to end (16 sts).
Beg with a p row, work in St st for 5 rows.
Change to B.
Dec row: (K2tog) to end (8 sts).
P 1 row.
Inc row: K1, (m1, k1) to end (15 sts).
P 1 row.
Inc row: K3, (m1, k3) to end (19 sts).
Beg with a p row, work in St st for 11 rows.
Change to A and work in St st for 10 rows.
Dec row: K3, (k2tog) twice, k5, (k2tog) twice, k3 (15 sts).
P 1 row.
Dec row: K2, (k2tog) twice, k3, (k2tog) twice, k2 (11 sts).
P 1 row.
Bind off.

Head
Note: Two separate balls of B are required.
Beg at center back using the thumb method and A, cast on 8 sts.
First and next foll 3 alt rows: P.
Inc row: (Inc) to end (16 sts).
Inc row: (K1, inc) to end (24 sts).
Inc row: (K2, inc) to end (32 sts).
Inc row: (K3, inc) to end (40 sts).
Beg with a p row, work in St st for 7 rows. Break yarn. Join on A and 2 balls of B as required and work in blocks of color, using a separate ball for each block and twisting when changing yarn.
Shape head
Row 1: K2tog, k7-B, k22-A, k7, k2tog tbl-B (second ball) (38 sts).
Row 2: P10-B, p18-A, p10-B.
Row 3: K2tog, k10-B, k14-A, k10, k2tog tbl-B (36 sts).
Row 4: P13-B, p10-A, p13-B.
Row 5: K2tog, k13-B, k6-A, k13, k2tog tbl-B (34 sts).
Row 6: P16-B, p2-A, p16-B.

giraffe

Row 7: K2tog, k to last 2 sts, k2tog tbl-B (first ball) (32 sts).
Row 8: P15-B, p2-A, p15-B.
Row 9: K2tog, k12-B, k4-A, k12, k2tog tbl-B (30 sts).
Row 10: P13-B, p4-A, p13-B.
Row 11: K2tog, k10-B, k6-A, k10, k2tog tbl-B (28 sts).
Row 12: P2tog tbl, p9-B, p6-A, p9, p2tog-B (26 sts).
Row 13: K2tog, k7-B, k8-A, k7, k2tog tbl-B (24 sts).
Row 14: P2tog tbl, p6-B, p8-A, p6, p2tog-B (22 sts).
Row 15: K2tog, k4-B, k10-A, k4, k2tog tbl-B (20 sts).
Row 16: P5-B, p10-A, p5-B.
Change to C.
Dec row: K3, (k2tog) twice, k6, (k2tog) twice, k3 (16 sts).
Beg with a p row, work in St st for 5 rows.
Dec row: K1, (k2tog, k1) to end (11 sts).
P 1 row.
Bind off.

Ears (make 2)

Using the thumb method and A, cast on 8 sts.
P 1 row.
Inc row: K1, (m1, k1) to end (15 sts).
Beg with a p row, work in St st for 3 rows.
Dec row: (K1, k2tog) to end (10 sts).
Beg with a p row, work in St st for 5 rows.
Dec row: (K2tog) to end (5 sts).
Thread yarn through rem sts, pull tight and secure.

Inside ear piece (make 2)

Using the thumb method and B, cast on 6 sts.
P 1 row.
Inc row: K2, (m1, k2) twice (8 sts).
Beg with a p row, work in St st for 3 rows.
Dec row: K2tog, k to last 2 sts, k2tog tbl.
Next row: P.
Rep last 2 rows once (4 sts).
Thread yarn through rem sts, pull tight and secure.

Horns (make 2)

Using the thumb method and A, cast on 8 sts.
Beg with a p row, work in St st for 4 rows ending on a k row.
Change to C and p 1 row.
Inc row: K1, (m1, k1) to end (15 sts).
Beg with a p row, work in St st for 3 rows.
Dec row: (K1, k2tog) to end (10 sts).
Thread yarn through rem sts and leave loose.

Mane

Special abbreviation: loop-st
Insert RH needle into next st, place first finger of LH behind LH needle and wind yarn around needle and finger twice, then just around needle once. Knit st, pulling 3 loops through. Place these loops on LH needle and knit into the back of them. Pull loops sharply down to secure. Cont to next st.
Using B, cast on 10 sts loosely.
First row: K1, (loop-st) to last st, k1.
K 1 row.
Rep first row once.
Bind off.

Tail

Note: Two separate balls of B are required.
Using the thumb method and A, cast on 15 sts.
Join in 2 balls of B and work in blocks of color, using a separate ball for each block and twisting when changing yarn.
Row 1: P2-B, p11-A, p2-B.
Row 2: K3-B, k9-A, k3-B.
Row 3: P4-B, p7-A, p4-B.
Row 4: K5-B, k5-A, k5-B.
Row 5: P6-B, p3-A, p6-B.
Row 6: K7-B, k1-A, k7-B.
Row 7: P across all sts-B (second ball).
Row 8: K7-B, k1-A, k7-B.
Row 9: P6-B, p3-A, p6-B.
Row 10: K5-B, k5-A, k5-B.
Row 11: P4-B, p7-A, p4-B.
Row 12: K3-B, k9-A, k3-B.
Row 13: P2-B, p11-A, p2-B.
Row 14: K 1 row-A.
Change to C and p 9 rows.
Dec row: (K1, k2tog) to end (10 sts).
Thread yarn through rem sts, pull tight and secure.

Assembly

Body

Place the two halves of body together matching all edges and join row-ends. Stuff body, leaving neck and lower edge open.

Base

Pin base to lower edge of body and sew all the way around, adding more stuffing if needed.

Hind legs

Gather cast-on sts of hooves, pull tight and secure. Stuff and join row-ends of hooves. Join row-ends of legs on right side using mattress stitch. Stuff legs. Place body on a flat surface, pin legs to body and sew bound-off sts of legs to body all the way around.

Forelegs

Work as for hind legs leaving gap to stuff. Stuff, close gap and with seam at center inside edge, whipstitch bound-off sts. Sew bound-off sts of forelegs to base of neck at each side.

Head

Join row ends of muzzle and with seam at center of underneath, join bound-off sts. Gather cast-on sts, pull tight and secure. Join row-ends leaving a gap, stuff and close gap. Pin head to body, adding more stuffing to neck if needed. Attach head to body by taking a small horizontal st from head, then a small horizontal st from body, alternating all the way around.

Ears

With wrong sides together, place inside ear piece down the center of ears, matching cast-on sts and allowing edges of ears to roll towards the center. Sew in place and attach ears to head at each side.

DID YOU KNOW?
The name "giraffe" comes from the Arabic word "zarafah" meaning "one who walks swiftly."

Horns

Roll each horn up from one set of row-ends to the other. Pull sts on thread tight and slip stitch in place. Attach horns to head between ears.

Embroidering the features

To make eyes, tie a knot in 2 lengths of black yarn winding yarn around 6 times to make each knot (see page 122). Check that the knots are the same size. Tie eyes to head halfway down, with 5 sts between. Weave ends into head. Embroider nostrils in black taking 2 long sts. To begin and fasten off invisibly for the embroidery, tie a knot in the end of yarn and take a large st through work coming up to begin embroidery. Allow knot to disappear through knitting and be caught in stuffing. To fasten off, sew a few sts back and forth through work, inserting the needle where the yarn comes out.

Mane

Join cast-on and bound-off sts of mane. Place across head behind ears and sew all edges of mane to head.

Tail

Join row-ends of tail and stuff. Sew cast-on sts to body at center back all the way around.

Each zebra has its unique stripe pattern—like human fingerprints. Some even have brown stripes. They also greet friends with a unique "smile." Members of the horse family, zebras can run at speeds of up to 35 miles per hour. They have excellent hearing and eyesight.

ZEBRA

What you'll need

Measurement
Zebra measures 9½in (24cm) in height

Materials
Any light worsted weight yarn:
175yd (1¾oz/50g) black (A)
175yd (1¾oz/50g) white (B)
Note: amounts are generous but
approximate
A pair of size 3 U.S. (3.25mm) needles
Polyester fiberfill
Straight pins

Gauge
26 sts x 34 rows measure 4in (10cm) square
over Stockinette st using size 3 U.S. needles
before stuffing

Abbreviations
See page 124

zebra

How to make Zebra

Body (make 2 pieces)

Beg at lower edge using the thumb method and A, cast on 35 sts.

First and next foll alt row: P.

Inc row: K10, m1, k15, m1, k10 (37 sts).

Join on B and work in stripe carrying yarn loosely up side of work, working the next 4 rows in B and then work 4 rows in A, alternating throughout while shaping as follows:

Inc row: K11, m1, k15, m1, k11 (39 sts).

Next and next 2 foll alt rows: P.

Inc row: K12, m1, k15, m1, k12 (41 sts).

Inc row: K13, m1, k15, m1, k13 (43 sts).

Inc row: K14, m1, k15, m1, k14 (45 sts).

Beg with a p row, work in St st for 9 rows.

Dec row: K2tog, k to last 2 sts, k2tog tbl.

Next row: P.

Rep last 2 rows 14 more times (15 sts).

Work in St st for 2 rows straight.

Bind off in A.

Base

Using the thumb method and A, cast on 20 sts.

First row: P.

Inc row: K1, m1, k to last st, m1, k1.

Rep first 2 rows 5 more times (32 sts).

Beg with a p row work in St st for 5 rows.

Dec row: K2tog, k to last 2 sts, k2tog tbl.

Next row: P.

Rep last 2 rows 5 more times (20 sts).

Bind off.

Hind legs (make 2)

Beg at hoof using the thumb method and A, cast on 6 sts.

First row: P.

Inc row: (Inc) to end.

Rep first 2 rows once (24 sts).

Next and next foll alt row: P.

Inc row: (K1, inc) to end (36 sts).

Garter st 2 rows.

Beg with a k row, work in St st for 2 rows.

Dec row: (K2, k2tog) to end (27 sts).

Beg with a p row work in St st for 3 rows.

Dec row: (K1, k2tog) to end (18 sts).

Beg with a p row work in St st for 3 rows.

Join on B and work in stripe carrying yarn loosely up side of work, working the next 4 rows in B and then work 4 rows in A, alternating throughout while shaping as follows:

Dec row: (K2tog) to end (9 sts).

P 1 row.

Inc row: K1, (m1, k1) to end (17 sts).

Beg with a p row, work in St st for 3 rows.

Inc row: K1, (m1, k1) to end (33 sts).

P 1 row.

Work 22 rows in stripe, beg with 4 rows B and finishing with 2 rows A.

Cont in A.

Dec row: (K1, k2tog) to end (22 sts).

P 1 row.

Bind off.

Forelegs (make 2)

Beg at hoof using the thumb method and A, cast on 6 sts.

First row: P.

Inc row: (Inc) to end.

Rep first 2 rows once (24 sts).

P 1 row.

Garter st 2 rows.

Beg with a k row, work in St st for 2 rows.

Dec row: (K1, k2tog) to end (16 sts).

Join on B and work in stripe carrying yarn loosely up side of work, working the next 4 rows in B and then work 4 rows in A, alternating throughout while shaping as follows:

Dec row: (K2tog) to end (8 sts).

P 1 row.

Inc row: K1, (m1, k1) to end (15 sts).

Beg with a p row, work in St st for 3 rows.

Inc row: K3, (m1, k3) to end (19 sts).

P 1 row.

Work 28 rows in stripe beg with 4 rows B and finishing with 4 rows B.

Continue in A.

Dec row: K3, (k2tog) twice, k5, (k2tog) twice, k3 (15 sts).

P 1 row.

Dec row: K2, (k2tog) twice, k3, (k2tog) twice, k2 (11 sts).

P 1 row.

Bind off in A.

Head

Beg at back of head using the thumb method and A, cast on 9 sts.

First and next 4 foll alt rows: P.

Inc row: (Inc) to end (18 sts).

Inc row: (K1, inc) to end (27 sts).

Inc row: (K2, inc) to end (36 sts).

Inc row: (K3, inc) to end (45 sts).

Inc row: (K4, inc) to end (54 sts).

Beg with a p row, work in St st for 5 rows.

Join on B and work in stripe carrying yarn loosely up side of work, working the next 4 rows in B and then work 4 rows in A, alternating throughout.

Work 12 rows in stripe.

Continue in stripe and decrease

Dec row: (K4, k2tog) to end (45 sts).

Beg with a p row, work in St st for 3 rows.

Dec row: (K3, k2tog) to end (36 sts).

Beg with a p row, work in St st for 3 rows.

Dec row: (K2, k2tog) to end (27 sts).

Beg with a p row, work in St st for 3 rows.

Cont in B.

Work in St st for 6 rows.

Dec row: K3, (k2tog) 4 times, k5, (k2tog) 4 times, k3 (19 sts).

P 1 row.

Bind off.

Ears (make 2)

Beg at lower edge using the thumb method and B, cast on 10 sts.
P 1 row.
Inc row: K2, (m1, k2) to end (14 sts).
Beg with a p row, work in St st for 2 rows, ending on a k row.
Change to A.
P 1 row.
Dec row: K2, (k2tog, k2) to end (11 sts).
Beg with a p row, work in St st for 3 rows.
Dec row: (K2tog) twice, k3, (k2tog) twice (7 sts).
Dec row: P1, (p2tog, p1) twice (5 sts).
Thread yarn through rem sts, pull tight and secure.

Mane

Special abbreviation: loop-st
Insert RH needle into next st, place first finger of LH behind LH needle and wind yarn around needle and finger twice, then just around needle once. Knit st, pulling 3 loops through. Place these loops on LH needle and knit into the back of them. Pull loops sharply down to secure. Cont to next st.
Using A, cast on 12 sts loosely.
First row: K1, (loop-st) to last st, k1.
K 1 row.
Rep first row once.
Bind off.

Tail

Beg at base using the thumb method and B, cast on 8 sts.
Beg with a p row, work in St st for 3 rows.
Join on A and work in stripe carrying yarn loosely up side of work.
Work in St st for 4 rows A.
Work in St st for 4 rows B.

Zebras have excellent eyesight and can even see in color. (Ironic, isn't it?)

Cont in A.
Garter st 7 rows.
Bind off k-wise.

Assembly

Body

Place the two halves of body together matching all edges and join row-ends. Stuff body leaving neck and lower edge open.

Base

Pin base to lower edge of body and sew base to body all the way around, adding more stuffing to base if needed.

Hind legs

Gather cast-on sts of hooves, pull tight and secure. Stuff and join row-ends of each hoof. Join row-ends of legs on right side using mattress stitch. Stuff legs. Place body on a flat surface, pin legs to body and sew bound-off sts of legs to body all the way around.

Forelegs

Work as for hind legs leaving gap to add stuffing. With seam at center of inside, whipstitch bound-off sts. Stuff and close gap and sew bound-off sts of forelegs to second black stripe down from neck at each side.

Head

Gather cast-on sts of head, pull tight then secure. Join row-ends leaving a gap and with seam at center of underneath, overcast bound-off sts. Stuff and close gap. Pin head to body adding more stuffing to neck if needed. Stitch head to body by taking a small horizontal st from head, then a small horizontal st from body, alternating all the way around.

Ears

Join row-ends of ears and with seams at center back, sew ears to white stripe on head with ears pointing outwards.

Embroidering the features

To make eyes, tie a knot in 2 lengths of black yarn winding the yarn around 6 times to make each knot (see page 122). Check that the knots are the same size. Tie eyes to white stripe of head with 7 knitted sts in between. Weave ends into head. Embroider nostrils in black taking 2 long sts. To begin and fasten off invisibly for the embroidery, tie a knot in the end of yarn and take a large st through work coming up to begin embroidery. Allow knot to disappear through knitting and be caught in stuffing. To fasten off, sew a few sts back and forth through work, inserting the needle where the yarn comes out.

Mane

Place mane across head behind ears and sew all edges of mane to head.

Tail

Join row-ends of tail and sew cast-on sts to first white stripe of body at center back all the way around.

The majority of a lion's time is taken up sleeping in trees or lying around.
Lions are great climbers and hunters. Their eyesight is five times better than a human's
and they can run the length of a football field in just six seconds.

LION

What you'll need

Measurement
Lion measures 9½in (24cm) in height

Materials
Any light worsted weight yarn:
350yd (3½oz/100g) golden-yellow (A)
175yd (1¾oz/50g) burnt-orange (B)
175yd (1¾oz/50g) brown (C)
Scrap of black for features
Note: amounts are generous but approximate
A pair of size 3 U.S. (3.25mm) needles
Polyester fiberfill
Straight pins

Gauge
26 sts x 34 rows measure 4in (10cm) square over Stockinette st using size 3 needles before stuffing

Abbreviations
See page 124

DID YOU KNOW? Lions make an art out of sleeping; sometimes they are only up for three hours a day.

How to make Lion

Body (make 2 pieces)
Beg at lower edge using the thumb method and A, cast on 35 sts.
First and next 4 foll alt rows: P.
Inc row: K10, m1, k15, m1, k10 (37 sts).
Inc row: K11, m1, k15, m1, k11 (39 sts).
Inc row: K12, m1, k15, m1, k12 (41 sts).
Inc row: K13, m1, k15, m1, k13 (43 sts).
Inc row: K14, m1, k15, m1, k14 (45 sts).
Beg with a p row, work in St st for 15 rows.
Dec row: K2tog, k to last 2 sts, k2tog tbl.
Next row: P.
Rep last 2 rows 12 more times (19 sts).
Bind off.

Base
Using the thumb method and A, cast on 20 sts.
First row: P.
Inc row: K1, m1, k to last st, m1, k1.
Rep first 2 rows 5 more times (32 sts).
Beg with a p row, work in St st for 5 rows.
Dec row: K2tog, k to last 2 sts, k2tog tbl.
Next row: P.
Rep last 2 rows 5 more times (20 sts).
Bind off.

Head
Beg at lower edge using the thumb method and A, cast on 9 sts.
First and next 5 foll alt rows: P.
Inc row: (Inc) to end (18 sts).
Inc row: (K1, inc) to end (27 sts).
Inc row: (K2, inc) to end (36 sts).
Inc row: (K3, inc) to end (45 sts).
Inc row: (K4, inc) to end (54 sts).
Inc row: (K5, inc) to end (63 sts).
Beg with a p row, work in St st for 19 rows.
Shape top of head
Dec row: (K5, k2tog) to end (54 sts).
Next and next 4 foll alt rows: P.
Dec row: (K4, k2tog) to end (45 sts).
Dec row: (K3, k2tog) to end (36 sts).
Dec row: (K2, k2tog) to end (28 sts).
Dec row: (K1, k2tog) to end (18 sts).

Dec row: (K2tog) to end (9 sts).
Thread yarn through rem sts, pull tight and secure.

Muzzle
First piece
Using the thumb method and A, cast on 12 sts.
Beg with a p row, work in St st for 3 rows.
Dec row: K1, k2tog, k to last 3 sts, k2tog tbl, k1.
Next row: P.
Rep last 2 rows 2 more times (6 sts).
Dec row: K1, k2tog, k2tog tbl, k1 (4 sts).
Thread yarn through rem sts, pull tight and secure.

Second piece
Using the thumb method and B, cast on 24 sts.
Beg with a p row, work in St st for 3 rows.
Dec row: (K1, k2tog, k6, k2tog tbl, k1) twice (20 sts).
Next and next 2 foll alt rows: P.
Dec row: (K1, k2tog, k4, k2tog tbl, k1) twice (16 sts).
Dec row: (K1, k2tog, k2, k2tog tbl, k1) twice (12 sts).
Dec row: (K1, k2tog, k2tog tbl, k1) twice (8 sts).
Thread yarn through rem sts and secure.

Hind legs (make 2)
Using the thumb method and A, cast on 32 sts.
Beg with a p row, work in St st for 13 rows.
Change to B.
Garter st 10 rows.
Dec row: (K2, k2tog) to end (24 sts).
Garter st 3 rows.
Dec row: (K1, k2tog) to end (16 sts).
K 1 row.
Dec row: (K2tog) to end (8 sts).
Thread yarn through rem sts, pull tight and secure.

Forelegs (make 2)
Using the thumb method and A, cast on 12 sts).
First row: Inc p-wise into every st (24 sts).
Work in St st for 26 rows.
Change to B.
Garter st 8 rows.
Dec row: (K1, k2tog) to end (16 sts).
Garter st 3 rows.
Dec row: (K2tog) to end (8 sts).
Thread yarn through rem sts, pull tight and secure.

Mane
Special abbreviation: loop-st
Insert RH needle into next st, place first finger of LH behind LH needle and wind yarn around needle and finger twice, then just around needle once. Knit st, pulling 3 loops through. Place these loops on LH needle and knit into the back of them. Pull loops down sharply to secure. Cont to next st.
Beg under chin using C, cast on 4 sts loosely.
Row 1: K1, (loop-st) to last st, k1.
Row 2: K.
Rows 3–7: Rep rows 1 and 2 twice, then row 1 again.
Row 8: K1, (inc) twice, k1 (6 sts).
Row 9: K1, (loop-st) to last st, k1.

Row 10: K.
Rows 11–15: Rep rows 9 and 10 twice, then row 9 again.
Row 16: K1, inc, k to last 2 sts, inc, k1.
Row 17: K1, (loop-st) to last st, k1.
Rows 18–25: Rep rows 16 and 17 4 times (16 sts).
Row 26: K.
Row 27: K1, (loop-st) to last st, k1.
Rows 28–51: Rep rows 26 and 27 12 times.
Row 52: K1, k2tog, k to last 2 sts, k2tog, k1.
Row 53: K1, (loop-st) to last st, k1.
Rows 54–61: Rep rows 52 and 53 4 times (6 sts).
Row 62: K.
Row 63: K1, (loop-st) to last st, k1.
Rows 64–67: Rep rows 62 and 63 twice.
Row 68: K1, (k2tog) twice, k1 (4 sts).
Row 69: K1, (loop-st) to last st, k1.
Row 70: K.
Rows 71–75: Rep rows 69 and 70 twice, then row 69 again.
Bind off.

Nose
Using the thumb method and black, cast on 6 sts.
P 1 row.
Dec row: K1, (k2tog) twice, k1 (4 sts).
Dec row: P1, p2tog, p1 (3 sts).
Thread yarn through rem sts, pull tight and secure.

Ears (make 2)
Beg at lower edge using the thumb method and A, cast on 8 sts.
P 1 row.
Inc row: K1, (m1, k1) to end (15 sts).
Beg with a p row, work in St st for 5 rows.
Dec row: (K1, k2tog) to end (10 sts).
Thread yarn through rem sts, pull tight and secure.

Tail
Using the thumb method and A, cast on 16 sts.
Beg with a p row, work in St st for 11 rows.
Change to B.
Garter st 8 rows.
Dec row: (K2tog) to end (8 sts).
Thread yarn through rem sts, pull tight and secure.

Assembly
Body
Place two halves of body together matching all edges and join row-ends. Stuff body leaving neck and lower edge open.

Base
Pin base to lower edge of body and sew base to body all the way around, adding more stuffing to base if needed.

Head
Gather cast-on sts of head, pull tight and secure. Join row-ends of head leaving gap, stuff and close gap. Pin head to body, adding more stuffing to neck if needed. Sew in place by taking a small horizontal st from head and then a small horizontal st from body, alternating all the way around.

Muzzle
Place right sides of muzzle pieces together matching sts pulled tight on a thread of both pieces. Join row-ends by sewing back and forth 1 st in from edge. Turn right-side out and stuff. Sew muzzle to center front of head, sewing lower edge of muzzle to neck.

Hind legs
Join row-ends of legs, leaving cast-on sts open, and stuff. Place body on a flat surface and pin and sew legs to body all the way around.

Forelegs
Join row-ends of forelegs and stuff. With seam at center of inside edge, whipstitch cast-on sts. Sew cast-on sts of each foreleg to either side of neck, and inside edge of forelegs to body.

Mane
Place mane on head joining under chin. Sew all edges down.

Nose
Place nose on muzzle and sew all edges down.

Ears
Join row-ends of ears. With seam at center back, part the mane and sew ears to head.

Tail
Join row-ends of tail. Stuff tail and sew to back of lion.

Embroidering the features
Embroider mouth in black as shown in picture. To begin and fasten off invisibly for the embroidery, tie a knot in end of yarn and take a large st through work, coming up to start the embroidery. Allow knot to disappear through knitting and be caught in stuffing. To fasten off, take a few sts back and forth through work, inserting needle where yarn comes out. To make eyes, tie a knot in 2 lengths of black yarn winding the yarn around 6 times to make each knot (see page 122). Check that the knots are the same size. Tie eyes to 5th row above muzzle with 7 knitted sts in between. Weave ends into head.

Giant pandas are native to China where they are called "large bear-cats." They spend at least 12 hours a day eating bamboo and will consume as much as 84 pounds of it. Although giant pandas seem pretty quiet, they bleat, roar, growl, honk, croak and squeal.

GIANT PANDA

What you'll need

Measurement
Giant panda measures 9½in (24cm) in height

Materials
Any light worsted weight yarn:
350yd (3½oz/100g) white (A)
350yd (3½oz/100g) black (B)
88yd (1oz/25g) beige (C)
88yd (1oz/25g) green (D)
Note: amounts are generous but approximate
A pair of size 3 U.S. (3.25mm) needles
Polyester fiberfill
Straight pins
Plastic drinking straw

Gauge
26 sts x 34 rows measure 4in (10cm) square over Stockinette st using size 3 needles before stuffing

Abbreviations
See page 124

How to make Giant panda

Body (make 2 pieces)

Beg at lower edge using the thumb method and A, cast on 35 sts.

First and next 4 foll alt rows: P.
Inc row: K10, m1, k15, m1, k10 (37 sts).
Inc row: K11, m1, k15, m1, k11 (39 sts).
Inc row: K12, m1, k15, m1, k12 (41 sts).
Inc row: K13, m1, k15, m1, k13 (43 sts).
Inc row: K14, m1, k15, m1, k14 (45 sts).
Beg with a p row, work in St st for 17 rows.
Dec row: K2tog, k to last 2 sts, k2tog tbl.
P 1 row.
Change to B.
Dec row: K2tog, k to last 2 sts, k2tog tbl.
Next row: P.
Rep last 2 rows 8 more times (25 sts).
Bind off.

Base

Using the thumb method and A, cast on 20 sts.
First row: P.
Inc row: K1, m1, k to last st, m1, k1.
Rep first 2 rows 5 more times (32 sts).
Beg with a p row, work in St st for 5 rows.
Dec row: K2tog, k to last 2 sts, k2tog tbl.
Next row: P.
Rep last 2 rows 5 more times (20 sts).
Bind off.

Head

Beg at lower edge using the thumb method and A, cast on 10 sts.
First and next 6 foll alt rows: P.
Inc row: (Inc) to end (20 sts).
Inc row: (K1, inc) to end (30 sts).
Inc row: (K2, inc) to end (40 sts).
Inc row: (K3, inc) to end (50 sts).
Inc row: (K4, inc) to end (60 sts).
Inc row: (K5, inc) to end (70 sts).
Inc row: (K6, inc) to end (80 sts).
Beg with a p row, work in St st for 15 rows.

Shape head

Dec row: (K8, k2tog) to end (72 sts).
Beg with a p row, work in St st for 3 rows.
Dec row: (K7, k2tog) to end (64 sts).
Beg with a p row, work in St st for 3 rows.
Dec row: (K6, k2tog) to end (56 sts).
Next and next 5 foll alt rows: P.
Dec row: (K5, k2tog) to end (48 sts).
Dec row: (K4, k2tog) to end (40 sts).
Dec row: (K3, k2tog) to end (32 sts).
Dec row: (K2, k2tog) to end (24 sts).
Dec row: (K1, k2tog) to end (16 sts).
Dec row: (K2tog) to end (8 sts).
Thread yarn through rem sts, pull tight and secure.

Hind legs (make 2)

Note: Follow individual instructions for right and left legs.

Beg at sole using the thumb method and B, cast on 22 sts.
Place a marker at center of cast-on sts.
P 1 row.
Inc row: K1, (m1, k1) to end (43 sts).
Beg with a p row, work in St st for 15 rows.
Dec for right leg: K4, (k2tog) 10 times, k19 (33 sts).
Dec for left leg: K19, (k2tog) 10 times, k4 (33 sts).
Beg with a p row, work in St st for 5 rows.
Cast off 9 sts at beg of next 2 rows (15 sts).
Dec row: (K2tog) twice, k to last 4 sts, k2tog, k2tog tbl (11 sts).
Dec row: P2tog tbl, p to last 2 sts, p2tog (9 sts). Bind off.

Arms (make 2)

Beg at shoulder using the thumb method and B, cast on 8 sts.

First and next foll alt row: P.

Inc row: (Inc) to end (16 sts).

Inc row: (K1, inc) to end (24 sts).

Beg with a p row, work in St st for 15 rows.

Shape elbow

Row 1: K4, turn.

Row 2: S1p, p to end.

Row 3: K6, turn.

Row 4: S1p, p to end.

Row 5: K8, turn.

Row 6: S1p, p to end.

Row 7: K10, turn.

Row 8: S1p, p to end.

Next row: K across all sts.

Shape second half of elbow

Row 1: P4, turn.

Row 2: S1k, k to end.

Row 3: P6, turn.

Row 4: S1k, k to end.

Row 5: P8, turn.

Row 6: S1k, k to end.

Row 7: P10, turn.

Row 8: S1k, k to end.

Next row: P across all sts.

Work in St st for 10 rows.

Dec row: (K1, k2tog) to end (16 sts).

P 1 row.

Dec row: (k2tog) to end (8 sts).

Thread yarn through rem sts, pull tight and secure.

Muzzle

Using the thumb method and A, cast on 30 sts.

Beg with a p row, work in St st for 3 rows.

Dec row: K2tog, k6, (k2tog) twice, k6, (k2tog) twice, k6, k2tog tbl (24 sts).

Next and next foll alt row: P.

Dec row: K2tog, k4, (k2tog) twice, k4 (k2tog) twice, k4, k2tog tbl (18 sts).

Dec row: K2tog, k2, (k2tog) twice, k2, (k2tog) twice, k2, k2tog tbl (12 sts).

P 1 row.

Thread yarn through sts, pull tight and secure.

Nose

Using the thumb method and B, cast on 6 sts.

P 1 row.

Dec row: K1, (k2tog) twice, k1 (4 sts).

Dec row: P1, p2tog, p1 (3 sts).

Thread yarn through rem sts, pull tight and secure.

Eye patches (make 2)

Note: Eye patches are worked in garter st.

Using the thumb method and B, cast on 6 sts.

Garter st 12 rows.

Dec row: K2tog, k to last 2 sts, k2tog tbl (4 sts).

Dec row: K1, k2tog, k1 (3 sts).

Thread yarn through rem sts, pull tight and secure.

Ears (make 2)

Using the thumb method and B, cast on 16 sts.

P 1 row.

Inc row: K1, (m1, k2) to last st, m1, k1 (24 sts).

Beg with a p row, work in St st for 7 rows.

Dec row: (K2, k2tog) to end (18 sts).

P 1 row.

Dec row: (K1, k2tog) to end (12 sts).

Dec row: (P2tog) to end (6 sts).

Thread yarn through rem sts, pull tight and secure.

Tail

Using the thumb method and A, cast on 10 sts.

P 1 row.

Inc row: K2, (m1, k2) to end (14 sts).

Next row: P.

Inc row: K1, m1, k to last st, m1, k1.

Rep last 2 rows once (18 sts).

P 1 row.

Cast on 3 sts at beg of next 2 rows, working the 4th st of each row tbl (24 sts).

Work in St st for 6 rows.

Dec row: (K1, k2tog) to end (16 sts).

P 1 row.

Dec row: (K2tog) to end (8 sts).

Thread yarn through rem sts, pull tight and secure.

Bamboo

Beg at lower edge using the thumb method and C, cast on 4 sts.

Inc row: Inc k-wise into each st (8 sts).

K 1 row.

Beg with a k row, work in St st for 2in (5cm), ending on a p row.

Garter st 4 rows.

Beg with a k row, work in St st for 3¼in (8cm), ending on a p row.

Garter st 2 rows.

Dec row: (K2tog) to end (4 sts).

Thread yarn through rem sts, pull tight and secure.

Leaves (make 6 pieces)

Using the thumb method and D, cast on 1 st.

Inc row: (K1, p1, k1) into first st (3 sts).

P 1 row.

Inc row: K1, m1, k1, m1, k1 (5 sts).

Beg with a p row, work in St st for 9 rows.

Dec row: K2tog, k1, k2tog tbl (3 sts).

Beg with a p row, work in St st for 3 rows.

Dec row: K3tog tbl (1 st).

Fasten off.

Assembly

Body
Place the two halves of body together matching all edges and join row-ends. Stuff body leaving neck and lower edge open.

Base
Pin base to lower edge of body and sew base to body all the way around, adding more stuffing to base if needed.

Head
Gather cast-on sts of head, pull tight and secure. Join row-ends of head leaving gap, stuff and close gap. Pin head to body adding more stuffing to neck if needed. Sew in place using black yarn by taking a small horizontal st from head and then a small horizontal st from body, alternating all the way around.

Hind legs
Join row-ends of hind legs and bring marker and seam together, whipstitch cast-on sts. Stuff legs, pushing stuffing into toes. Stand body on flat surface and pin legs to body. Sew legs to body all the way around.

Arms
Gather cast-on sts at shoulder, pull tight and secure. Join row-ends of arms leaving gap, stuff and close gap. Sew arms to body at each side.

Muzzle
Join row-ends of muzzle and stuff. Pin and sew muzzle to face.

Nose
Place nose onto the muzzle and then sew all edges down.

Ears
Join row-ends of ears and with seam at center back, sew ears to head.

Tail
Join row-ends of tail from sts on a thread to bound-off sts. Stuff and sew to back of panda.

Eye patches
Sew eye patches to face around muzzle.

Embroidering the features
Embroider a circle of white for each eye using chain stitch. Embroider mouth in black as shown in photograph. To begin and fasten off invisibly for the embroidery, tie a knot in end of yarn and take a large st through work, coming up to start the embroidery. Allow knot to disappear through knitting and be caught in stuffing. To fasten off, take a few sts back and forth through work, inserting needle where yarn comes out.

Bamboo
Gather cast-on sts of bamboo, pull tight and secure. Cut an extra wide drinking straw to 6¼in (16cm) and enclose straw in knitting by joining row-ends of bamboo around it.

Leaves
Make 3 leaves by placing wrong sides of 2 pieces together, matching all edges and sew around edge. Sew leaves to bamboo as shown in photograph.

DID YOU KNOW? Pandas are pink when they are born. The black markings develop after about a month.

In many cultures the tiger is a symbol of strength and courage. They are the largest of the big cats with night vision six times greater than a human's. The pattern of their stripes is like the human fingerprint, unique to each individual.

TIGER

Tigers, like most cats, enjoy a good rest.

What you'll need

Measurement
Tiger measures 9½in (24cm) in height

Materials
Any light worsted weight yarn:
350yd (3½oz/100g) orange (A)
175yd (1¾oz/50g) black (B)
70yd (1oz/20g) cream (C)
Scrap of gray for features

Note: amounts are generous but approximate

A pair of size 3 U.S. (3.25mm) needles
Polyester fiberfill
Straight pins

Gauge
26 sts x 34 rows measure 4in (10cm) square
over Stockinette st using size 3 U.S. needles
before stuffing

Abbreviations
See page 124

Pattern notes
Before beginning to knit, wind yarns
A and B into two separate balls.

Tigers are shy.

How to make Tiger

Body (make 2 pieces)
Note: Two separate balls of A are required. Beg at lower edge using the thumb method and first ball of A, cast on 35 sts.
P 1 row.
Join in B and second ball of A and work in St st in stripe, carrying yarn loosely up sides of work.
Row 1: Using A, k10, m1, k15, m1, k10 (37 sts).
Row 2: Using A, p.
Row 3: Using B, k11, m1, k15, m1, k11 (39 sts).
Row 4: Using A (second ball), p.
Row 5: Using A, k12, m1, k15, m1, k12 (41 sts).
Row 6: Using B, p.
Row 7: Using A, k13, m1, k15, m1, k13 (43 sts).
Row 8: Using A, p.
Row 9: Using A, k14, m1, k15, m1, k14 (45 sts).
Row 10: Using A, p.
Row 11: Using B, k.
Rows 12 and 13: Using A, work in St st for 2 rows.
Row 14: Using B, p.
Rows 15–18: Using A, work in St st for 4 rows.
Row 19: Using B, k.
Rows 20 and 21: Using A, work in St st for 2 rows.
Row 22: Using B, p.

Shape sides
Row 23: Using A, k2tog, k to last 2 sts, k2tog tbl (43 sts).
Row 24: Using A, p.
Row 25: Using A, k2tog, k to last 2 sts, k2tog tbl (41 sts).
Row 26: Using A, p.
Cont in stripe as set for 22 more rows, dec 1 st at each end of next and every foll alt row (19 sts).
Bind off in A.

Base
Using the thumb method and A, cast on 20 sts.
First row: P.
Inc row: K1, m1, k to last st, m1, k1.
Rep first 2 rows 5 more times (32 sts).
Beg with a p row, work in St st for 5 rows.
Dec row: K2tog, k to last 2 sts, k2tog tbl.
Next row: P.
Rep last 2 rows 5 more times (20 sts).
Bind off.

Head
Note: Two separate balls of A are required. Beg at center back using the thumb method and first ball of A, cast on 8 sts.
P 1 row.

Join on B and second ball of A and work in St st in stripe, carrying yarn loosely up sides of work.
Row 1: Using A, k1, (m1, k1) to end (15 sts).
Row 2: Using A, p.
Row 3: Using B, k1, (m1, k2) to end (22 sts).
Row 4: Using A (second ball), p.
Row 5: Using A, k1, (m1, k3) to end (29 sts).
Row 6: Using B, p.
Row 7: Using A, k1, (m1, k4) to end (38 sts).
Row 8: Using A, p.
Row 9: Using A, k1, (m1, k5) to end (43 sts).
Row 10: Using A, p.
Row 11: Using B, k1, (m1, k6) to end (50 sts).
Row 12: Using A, p.
Row 13: Using A, k1, (m1, k7) to end (57 sts).
Row 14: Using B, p.
Row 15: Using A, k1, (m1, k8) to end (64 sts).
Keeping stripe patt correct and beg with a p row, work in St st for 23 rows, ending with 10th black stripe.
Cont with 1 ball of A.

Shape face
Dec row: Using A, (k6, k2tog) to end (56 sts).
Next row: Using A, p.
Dec row: Using A, (k5, k2tog) to end (48 sts).
Next row: Using A, p.
Dec row: Using B, (k4, k2tog) to end (40 sts).
Next row: Using A, p.
Dec row: Using A, (k3, k2tog) to end (32 sts).
Next row: Using B, p.
Cont with 1 ball of A.
Dec row: (K2, k2tog) to end (24 sts).
Next row and next foll alt row: P.
Dec row: (K1, k2tog) to end (16 sts).
Dec row: (K2tog) to end (8 sts).
Thread yarn through rem sts, pull tight and secure.

Muzzle

First piece

Using the thumb method and A, cast on 12 sts.

Beg with a p row, work in St st for 3 rows.

Dec row: K1, k2tog, k to last 3 sts, k2tog tbl, k1.

Next row: P.

Rep last 2 rows twice more (6 sts).

Dec row: K1, k2tog, k2tog tbl, k1 (4 sts).

Thread yarn through rem sts, pull tight and secure.

Second piece

Using the thumb method and C, cast on 24 sts.

Beg with a p row, work in St st for 3 rows.

Dec row: (K1, k2tog, k6, k2tog tbl, k1) twice (20 sts).

Next and next 2 foll alt rows: P.

Dec row: (K1, k2tog, k4, k2tog tbl, k1) twice (16 sts).

Dec row: (K1, k2tog, k2, k2tog tbl, k1) twice (12 sts).

Dec row: (K1, k2tog, k2tog tbl, k1) twice (8 sts).

Thread yarn through rem sts, pull tight and secure.

Hind legs (make 2)

Note: Two separate balls of A are required. Using the thumb method and A, cast on 40 sts.

P 1 row.

Join on B and second ball of A and work in St st in stripe, carrying yarn loosely up sides of work.

Row 1: Using B, k.

Rows 2 and 3: Using A (second ball) work in St st, beg with a p row.

Row 4: Using B, p.

Rows 5–8: Using A, work in St st for 4 rows.

Rows 9–16: As rows 1–8.

Cont in B.

Work in St st for 4 rows.

Dec row: (K3, k2tog) to end (32 sts).

Next and next 2 foll alt rows: P.

Dec row: (K2, k2tog) to end (24 sts).

Dec row: (K1, k2tog) to end (16 sts).

Dec row: (K2tog) to end (8 sts).

Thread yarn through rem sts, pull tight and secure.

Forelegs (make 2)

Note: Two separate balls of A are required. Using the thumb method and A, cast on 15 sts.

Row 1: Inc p-wise into every st (30 sts).

Join in B and second ball of A and work in St st in stripe, carrying yarn loosely up sides of work.

Stripe pattern

Row 1: Using B, k.

Rows 2 and 3: Using A (second ball), beg with a p row, work in St st for 2 rows.

Row 4: Using B, p.

Rows 5–8: Using A, work in St st for 4 rows.

Rows 9–24: As rows 1–8 twice.

Using B, work in St st for 6 rows.

Dec row: (K1, k2tog) to end (20 sts).

P 1 row.

Dec row: (K2tog) to end (10 sts).

Dec row: (P2tog) to end (5 sts).

Thread yarn through rem sts, pull tight and secure.

Nose

Using the thumb method and B, cast on 6 sts.

P 1 row.

Dec row: K1, (k2tog) twice, k1 (4 sts).

Dec row: P1, p2tog, p1 (3 sts).

Thread yarn through rem sts, pull tight and secure.

Ears (make 2)

First piece

Note: Two separate balls of B are required. Beg at lower edge using the thumb method and A and B, cast on 3 sts in B, 6 sts in A and 3 sts in B (second ball), all on the same needle (12 sts).

Work in blocks of color using a separate ball of yarn for each block and twisting when changing yarn.

First row: P3-B, p6-A, p3-B.

Next row: K3-B, k6-A, k3-B.

Rep first row once.

Dec row: K3-B, k2tog, k2, k2tog tbl-A, k3-B (10 sts).

Next row: P3-B, p4-A, p3-B.

Dec row: K3-B, k2tog, k2tog tbl-A, k3-B (8 sts).

Next row: P3-B, p2-A, p3-B.

Cont with 1 ball of B.

Dec row: K3, k2tog, k3 (7 sts).

Dec row: P2, p3tog, p2 (5 sts).

Dec row: K1, k3tog, k1 (3 sts).

Thread yarn through rem sts, pull tight and secure.

Second piece

Beg at lower edge using B, cast on 11 sts.

Beg with a p row work in St st for 3 rows.

Dec row: K1, k2tog, k to last 3 sts, k2tog tbl, k1.

Next row: P.

Rep last 2 rows twice more (5 sts).

Dec row: K1, k3tog, k1 (3 sts).

Thread yarn through rem sts, pull tight and secure.

Tail

Note: Two separate balls of A are required.
Using the thumb method and first ball of
A, cast on 18 sts.
P 1 row.
Join in B and second ball of A and work in
St st in stripe, carrying yarn loosely up
sides of work.
Rows 1 and 2: Using A, beg with a k row,
work in St st for 2 rows.
Row 3: Using B, k.
Rows 4 and 5: Using A (second ball),
work in St st for 2 rows beg with a p row.
Row 6: Using B, p.
Row 7: Using A, k.
Row 8: Using A, p8, turn.
Row 9: Using A, s1k, k to end.
Row 10: Using A, p.
Row 11: Using A, k8, turn.
Row 12: Using A, s1p, p to end.
Row 13: Using B, k.
Row 14 and 15: Using A, beg with a p row,
work in St st for 2 rows.
Row 16: Using B, p.
Rows 17–26: As rows 7–16 once.
Cont with 1 ball of A.
Next and next foll alt row: K.
Dec row: (P1, p2tog) to end (12 sts).
Dec row: (P2tog) to end (6 sts).Thread yarn
through rem sts, pull tight and secure.

Assembly

Body

Place two halves of body together matching
all edges and join row-ends by sewing back
and forth 1 st in from edge. Stuff body
leaving neck and lower edge open.

Base

Pin base to lower edge of body and sew
base to body all the way around, adding
more stuffing to base if needed.

Head

Gather cast-on sts of head, pull tight
and secure. Join row-ends of head leaving
gap, stuff and close gap. Pin head to body,
adding more stuffing to neck if needed.
With sts pulled tight on a thread at center
front and cast-on sts at center back, sew in
place by taking a small horizontal st from
head and then a small horizontal st from
body, alternating all the way around.

Muzzle

Place right sides of both pieces of muzzle
together matching sts pulled tight on a
thread of both pieces. Join row-ends by
sewing back and forth 1 st in from edge.
Turn right-side out and stuff. Sew muzzle
to lower half of head at center front.

Hind legs

Join row-ends of hind legs on wrong side
by sewing back and forth 1 st in from edge.
Leaving cast-on sts open, stuff. Place body
on a flat surface and pin and sew legs to
body all the way around.

Forelegs

Join row-ends of forelegs on wrong side
by sewing back and forth 1 st in from
edge. Stuff, and with seam at center of
inside edge, whipstitch cast-on sts. Sew
cast-on sts of each foreleg to neck either
side of body, and inside edge of forelegs
to halfway down body.

Nose

Place nose on muzzle and sew all edges
down.

Ears

Place right sides of first and second ear
pieces together and join row-ends by
sewing back and forth 1 st in from edge.
Turn right-side out and sew lower edges
of ears to head.

Tail

Join row-ends of tail from sts on a thread
to bound-off sts, by sewing back and forth
1 st in from edge. Leaving cast-on sts open,
stuff and, with tip of tail curling upwards,
sew to back of tiger with seam underneath.

Embroidering the features

Embroider mouth in black as shown in
photograph. To begin and fasten off invisibly
for the embroidery, tie a knot in end of yarn
and take a large st through work, coming
up to start the embroidery. Allow knot to
disappear through knitting and be caught
in stuffing. To fasten off, take a few sts back
and forth through work, inserting needle
where yarn comes out. To make eyes, tie
a knot in 2 lengths of gray yarn, winding
the yarn around 6 times to make each knot
(see page 122). Check that the knots are
the same size. Tie eyes to 5th row above
muzzle with 8 knitted sts in between.
Weave ends into head.

Tigers can eat 100 pounds of meat in one sitting.
That's like eating 400 hamburgers for dinner!

Crocodiles are most at home in or near the water. They can swim up to 20 miles per hour and hold their breath underwater for more than an hour. They are very fast over short distances, even out of water, and can reach speeds of 11 miles per hour when they "belly run." Crocodiles also have exceptional hearing. They can even hear their young calling from inside their eggshells!

CROCODILE

What you'll need

Measurement
Crocodile measures 19in (48cm) from head to tail

Materials
Any light worsted weight yarn:
350yd (3½oz/100g) green (A)
70yd (¾oz/20g) white (B)
70yd (¾oz/20g) black (C)
Note: amounts are generous but approximate
A pair of size 3 U.S. (3.25mm) needles
Polyester fiberfill
Straight pins

Gauge
26 sts x 34 rows measure 4in (10cm) square over Stockinette st using size 3 U.S. needles before stuffing

Abbreviations
See page 124
Special abbreviation: Seed st
Beg with a k st, k1, (p1, k1) to end
This row is repeated

DID YOU KNOW? A crocodile cannot stick its tongue out, however much it may want to.

How to make Crocodile

Body and head

Beg at tail using the thumb method and A, cast on 7 sts.

P 1 row.

Row 1: K1, (m1, k1) to end (13 sts).
Row 2: P5, work in seed st for 3, p5.
Row 3: K3, work in seed st for 7, k3.
Row 4: As row 2.
Row 5: K3, (m1, k1) twice, work in seed st for 3, (m1, k1) twice, k3 (17 sts).
Row 6: P5, work in seed st for 7, p5.
Row 7: K5, work in seed st for 7, k5.
Row 8: As row 6.
Row 9: As row 7.
Row 10: As row 6.
Row 11: K3, (m1, k1) twice, work in seed st for 7, (m1, k1) twice, k3 (21 sts).
Row 12: P7, work in seed st for 7, p7.
Row 13: K7, work in seed st for 7, k7.
Row 14: As row 12.
Row 15: As row 13.
Row 16: As row 12.
Row 17: K5, (m1, k1) twice, work in seed st for 7, (m1, k1) twice, k5 (25 sts).
Row 18: P7, work in seed st for 11, p7.
Row 19: K7, work in seed st for 11, k7.
Row 20: As row 18.
Row 21: As row 19.
Row 22: As row 18.
Row 23: K5, (m1, k1) twice, work in seed st for 11, (m1, k1) twice, k5 (29 sts).
Row 24: P9, work in seed st for 11, p9.
Row 25: K9, work in seed st for 11, k9.
Row 26: As row 24.
Row 27: As row 25.
Row 28: As row 24.
Row 29: K7, (m1, k1) twice, work in seed st for 11 sts, (m1, k1) twice, k7 (33 sts).
Row 30: P9, work in seed st for 15, p9.
Row 31: K9, work in seed st for 15, k9.

Row 32: As row 30.
Row 33: As row 31.
Row 34: As row 30.
Row 35: K7, (m1, k1) twice, work in seed st for 15, (m1, k1) twice, k7 (37 sts).
Row 36: P11, work in seed st for 15, p11.
Row 37: K11, work in seed st for 15, k11.
Row 38: As row 36.
Row 39: As row 37.
Row 40: As row 36.
Row 41: K9, (m1, k1) twice, work in seed st for 15, (m1, k1) twice, k9 (41 sts).
Row 42: P11, work in seed st for 19, p11.
Row 43: K11, work in seed st for 19, k11.
Row 44: As row 42.
Row 45: As row 43.
Row 46: As row 42.
Row 47: K9, (m1, k1) twice, work in seed st for 19, (m1, k1) twice, k9 (45 sts).
Row 48: P13, work in seed st for 19, p13.
Row 49: K13, work in seed st for 19, k13.
Row 50: As row 48.
Row 51: As row 49.
Row 52: As row 48.
Row 53: K11, (m1, k1) twice, work in seed st for 19, (m1, k1) twice, k11 (49 sts).
Row 54: P13, work in seed st for 23, p13.
Row 55: K13, work in seed st for 23, k13.
Row 56: As row 54.
Row 57: As row 55.
Row 58: As row 54.
Row 59: K11, (m1, k1) twice, work in seed st for 23, (m1, k1) twice, k11 (53 sts).
Row 60: P15, work in seed st for 23, p15.

Row 61: K15, work in seed st for 23, k15.
Row 62: As row 60.
Row 63: As row 61.
Row 64: As row 60.
Row 65: K13, (m1, k1) twice, work in seed st for 23, (m1, k1) twice, k13 (57 sts).
Row 66: P15, work in seed st for 27, p15.
Row 67: K15, work in seed st for 27, k15.
Row 68: As row 66.
Row 69: As row 67.
Row 70: As row 66.
Row 71: K13, (m1, k1) twice, work in seed st for 27, (m1, k1) twice, k13 (61 sts).
Row 72: P17, work in seed st for 27, p17.
Row 73: K17, work in seed st for 27, k17.
Row 74: As row 72.
Row 75: As row 73.
Row 76: As row 72.
Row 77: K15, (m1, k1) twice, work in seed st for 27, (m1, k1) twice, k15 (65 sts).
Row 78: P17, work in seed st for 31, p17.
Row 79: K17, work in seed st for 31, k17.
Row 80: P17, work in seed st for 31, k17.
Rep rows 79 and 80 30 more times.
Dec row: K16, k3tog tbl, work in seed st for 27, k3tog, k16 (61 sts).
Next row: P17, work in seed st for 27, p17.
Next row: K17, work in seed st for 27, k17.
Next row: P17, work in seed st for 27, p17.
Dec row: K16, k3tog tbl, work in seed st for 23, k3tog, k16 (57 sts).
Next row: P17, work in seed st for 23, p17.
Next row: K17, work in seed st for 23, k17.
Next row: P17, work in seed st for 23, p17.
Dec row: K16, k3tog tbl, work in seed st for 19, k3tog, k16 (53 sts).
Next row: P17, work in seed st for 19, p17.
Next row: K17, work in seed st for 19, k17.
Next row: P17, work in seed st for 19, p17.
Dec row: K16, k3tog tbl, work in seed st for 15, k3tog, k16 (49 sts).
Beg with a p row, work in St st for 21 rows.
Dec row: K7, (k3, k2tog) 7 times, k7 (42 sts).
P 1 row.

Dec row: K7, (k2, k2tog) 7 times, k7 (35 sts).
Beg with a p row, work in St st for 3 rows.
Dec row: K7, (k1, k2tog) 7 times, k7 (28 sts).
Beg with a p row, work in St st for 19 rows.
Dec row: (K2, k2tog) to end (21 sts).
P 1 row.
Dec row: (K1, k2tog) to end (14 sts).
Dec row: (P2tog) to end (7 sts).

Legs (make 4)
Beg at lower edge using the thumb method
and A, cast on 14 sts.
Inc row: (K1, inc) to end (21 sts).
Cont in work in seed st.
Work in seed st for 7 rows.
Shape gusset
Dec row: K2tog, work in seed st for to last
2 sts, k2tog tbl.
Dec row: K1, p2tog, work in seed st for to
last 3 sts, p2tog, k1.
Work in seed st for 2 rows.
Rep last 4 rows once (13 sts).
Inc row: K1, inc k-wise into next st, work
in seed st for to last 2 sts, inc k-wise, k1.
Inc row: Inc k-wise into first st, work in
seed st for to last st, inc k-wise.
Work in seed st for 2 rows.
Rep last 4 rows once (21 sts).
Work in seed st for 6 rows.
Dec row: K1, (p3tog, k1) to end (11 sts).
Work in seed st for 1 row.
Thread yarn through sts, pull tight and secure.

Feet (make 8 pieces)
Note: Feet are worked in garter st.
Using the thumb method and A, cast on
18 sts.
Row 1: K.
Row 2: K6 turn.
Row 3: S1k, k to end.
Row 4: Bind off 5 sts at beg of next row
(13 sts).
Row 5: K.

Row 6: Bind on 5 sts at beg of next row
and k the 6th st of row tbl (18 sts).
Rep rows 1–6 once.
Next row: K.
Next row: K6, turn.
Next row: S1k, k to end.
Bind off loosely in garter st.

Eyes (make 2)
Using the thumb method and B, cast on
6 sts.
P 1 row.
Inc row: (Inc) to end (12 sts).
Beg with a p row, work in St st for 3 rows.
Change to C.
Work in St st for 3 rows, ending on a k row.
Thread yarn through sts, pull tight
and secure.

Eyelids (make 2)
Using the thumb method and A, cast on
10 sts.
Beg with a p row, work in St st for 2 rows,
ending on a k row.
Dec row: (P2tog) to end (5 sts).
Thread yarn through rem sts, pull tight
and secure.

Assembly
Body and head
Join row-ends of head and stuff. Join
row-ends of body beginning at tail and
stuff lightly as you go, keeping body flat.

Legs and feet
Join straight row-ends of legs above and
below the gusset. Bring gusset together
horizontally and overcast. Stuff legs and fold
cast-on sts in half and whipstitch. Take 2
pieces of feet and place together, matching
all edges. Whipstitch edges, sewing cast-on
and bound-off sts together and sew
around toes.

Push a small amount of stuffing inside and
gather straight row-ends, pull tight and then
secure. Sew feet to lower edge of legs. Place
crocodile on a flat surface and assemble legs.
Sew legs to body.

Eyes
Join row-ends of eyes and gather cast-on
sts, pull tight and secure. Press eyes flat,
like a button, and sew to head, with seam
under eyelid.

Eyelids
Sew eyelids to head, overlapping eyes.
Sew cast-on sts of lids to eyes.

Embroidering the features
Using black, embroider a curving mouth
in chain stitch. Embroider 2 long sts in
black as nostrils at end of snout. Embroider
teeth in white, taking uneven straight sts
along mouth, starting and finishing invisibly
for embroidery (see page 122).

There are 125 different species of monkey. The loudest are howler monkeys, which can be heard more than 3 miles away. All monkeys love to eat bananas. Some species have cheek pouches, so they can stuff the fruit in on the run for later. Colobus monkeys see burping as a friendly social gesture.

MONKEY

What you'll need

Measurement
Monkey measures 12½in (32cm) in height

Materials
Any light worsted weight yarn:
350yd (3½oz/100g) brown (A)
175yd (1¾oz/50g) beige (B)
88yd (1oz/25g) yellow (C)
88yd (1oz/25g) cream (D)
Scrap of black for features
Note: amounts are generous but
approximate
A pair of size 3 U.S. (3.25mm) needles
Polyester fiberfill
Straight pins
Tweezers for stuffing small parts (optional)

Gauge
26 sts x 34 rows measure 4in (10cm) square
over Stockinette st using size 3 U.S. needles
before stuffing

Abbreviations
See page 124

DID YOU KNOW? A monkey was once tried and convicted for smoking a cigarette in South Bend, Indiana, USA.

monkey

How to make Monkey

Body (make 2 pieces)

Beg at lower edge using the thumb method and A, cast on 24 sts.

First and next foll 3 alt rows: P.

Inc row: K5, m1, k14, m1, k5 (26 sts).

Inc row: K6, m1, k14, m1, k6 (28 sts).

Inc row: K7, m1, k14, m1, k7 (30 sts).

Inc row: K8, m1, k14, m1, k8 (32 sts).

Beg with a p row, work in St st for 19 rows.

Dec row: K2tog, k to last 2 sts, k2tog tbl.

Next row: P.

Rep last 2 rows 8 times more (14 sts).

Bind off.

Base

Using the thumb method and A, cast on 14 sts.

First row: P.

Inc row: K1, m1, k to last st, m1, k1.

Rep first 2 rows 2 more times (20 sts).

Beg with a p row, work in St st for 5 rows.

Dec row: K2tog, k to last 2 sts, k2tog tbl.

P 1 row.

Rep last 2 rows twice more (14 sts).

Bind off.

Head

Beg at lower edge using the thumb method and A, cast on 9 sts.

First and next 4 foll alt rows: P.

Inc row: (Inc) to end (18 sts).

Inc row: (K1, inc) to end (27 sts).

Inc row: (K2, inc) to end (36 sts).

Inc row: (K3, inc) to end (45 sts).

Inc row: (K4, inc) to end (54 sts).

Beg with a p row, work in St st for 17 rows.

Shape top of head

Dec row: (K4, k2tog) to end (45 sts).

Beg with a p row, work in St st for 3 rows.

Dec row: (K3, k2tog) to end (36 sts).

Next and next 2 foll alt rows: P.

Dec row: (K2, k2tog) to end (27 sts).

Dec row: (K1, k2tog) to end (18 sts).

Dec row: (K2tog) to end (9 sts).

Thread yarn through rem sts, pull tight and secure.

Muzzle

Using the thumb method and B, cast on 28 sts.

P 1 row.

Inc row: K1, (m1, k2) to last st, m1, k1 (44 sts).

Beg with a p row, work in St st for 3 rows.

Dec row: K2, (k2tog, k2) to end (32 sts).

Beg with a p row, work in St st for 3 rows.

Dec row: K2, (k2tog) 6 times, k4, (k2tog) 6 times, k2, (20 sts).

P 1 row.

Bind off.

Eye piece

Beg at lower edge using the thumb method and B, cast on 12 sts.

P 1 row.

Inc row: K1, m1, k to last st, m1, k1 (14 sts).

Beg with a p row, work in St st for 3 rows.

Next row: K7.

Turn and work on these 7 sts.

P 1 row.

Dec row: K2tog, k to last 2 sts, k2tog tbl (5 sts).

Dec row: P2tog tbl, p1, p2tog (3 sts).

Break yarn and thread through sts, pull tight and secure.

Rejoin yarn to rem sts and k 1 row (7 sts).

Complete to match first side.

Ears (make 2)

Using the thumb method and B, cast on 12 sts.

Beg with a p row, work in St st for 5 rows.

Dec row: (K2tog) to end (6 sts).

Thread yarn through rem sts, pull tight and secure.

Legs (make 2)

Using the thumb method and A, cast on 20 sts.

Beg with a p row, work in St st for 45 rows.

Cast off.

Feet (make 2)

Using the thumb method and B, cast on 18 sts.

P 1 row.

Inc row: K2, (m1, k2) to end (26 sts).

Beg with a p row, work in St st for 5 rows.

Inc row: K1, m1, k to last st, m1, k1 (28 sts).

Beg with a p row, work in St st for 7 rows

Shape big toe

Bind off 4 sts at beg of next 2 rows (20 sts).

Work in St st for 4 rows.

Dec row: (K2tog) to end (10 sts).

P 1 row.

Dec row: (K2tog) to end (5 sts).

Thread yarn through rem sts, pull tight and secure.

Hands and arms (make 2)

Beg at shoulder using the thumb method and A, cast on 12 sts.

Beg with a p row, work in St st for 5 rows.

Inc row: K1, m1, k to last st, m1, k1.

Rep last 6 rows 3 times more (20 sts).

Beg with a p row, work in St st for 9 rows.

Inc row: K1, m1, k to last st, m1, k1.

Rep last 10 rows once (24 sts).

P 1 row.

Change to B for hand.

Work in St st for 2 rows.

Inc row: K1, m1, k to last st, m1, k1
(26 sts).
Beg with a p row, work in St st for 5 rows.
Shape thumb
Cast off 4 sts at beg of next 2 rows (18 sts).
Work in St st for 4 rows.
Dec row: (K1, k2tog) to end
(12 sts).
Dec row: (P2tog) to end (6 sts).
Thread yarn through rem sts, pull tight
and secure.

Tail

Using B, cast on 8 sts.
Work in St st until tail measures
9½in (24cm).
Thread yarn through sts, pull tight
and secure.

Banana

Beg at lower edge using the thumb
method and C, cast on 6 sts.
First and next 2 foll alt rows: P.
Inc row: (K1, inc) to end (9 sts).
Inc row: (K2, inc) to end (12 sts).
Inc row: (K3, inc) to end (15 sts).
Beg with a p row, work in St st for 7 rows.
Change to D and work in St st for 6 rows.
Dec row: (K3, k2tog) to end (12 sts).
Next and next foll alt row: P.
Dec row: (K2, k2tog) to end (9 sts).
Dec row: (K1, k2tog) to end (6 sts).
Thread yarn through rem sts, pull tight
and secure.

Skins (make 3)

Using the thumb method and C, cast
on 8 sts.
Beg with a p row, work in St st for 3 rows.
Dec row: K2, (k2tog) twice, k2 (6 sts).
Next and next foll alt row: P.
Dec row: K1, (k2tog) twice, k1 (4 sts).
Dec row: K2tog, k2tog tbl (2 sts).
Thread yarn through rem sts, pull tight
and secure.

Skin linings (make 3)

Using the thumb method and D, cast
on 6 sts.
Beg with a p row, work in St st for 3 rows.
Dec row: K1, (k2tog) twice, k1 (4 sts).
P 1 row.
Dec row: K2tog, k2tog tbl (2 sts).
Thread yarn through rem sts, pull tight
and secure.

Assembly
Body

Place the two halves of body together
matching all edges and join row-ends. Stuff
body leaving neck and lower edge open.

Base

Pin base to lower edge of body and sew
base to body all the way around, adding
more stuffing to base if needed.

Head

Gather cast-on sts of head, pull tight
and secure. Join row-ends leaving a gap,
stuff and close gap. Pin head to body,
adding more stuffing to neck if needed,
and stitch head in place by taking a small
horizontal st from head and then a small
horizontal st from body, alternating all the
way around.

Legs and feet

Join row ends of legs and stuff. Fold feet in
half and join row-ends and stuff. Whipstitch
cast-on sts of feet and sew feet to legs with
both big toes pointing inwards. Sew legs
to body.

Hands and arms

Fold bound-off sts of hands in half and join
row-ends of hands and sew around thumb.
Stuff hands. Fold cast-on sts of arms in
half and overcast. Join row-ends of arms,
starting at shoulder using mattress stitch,
stuffing as you go. With thumbs pointing
forwards, sew top of arms to 4th row below
neck at either side.

Muzzle

Join row-ends of muzzle and with this seam
at center of underneath, join bound-off sts.
Stuff, then pin and sew muzzle to lower half
of head at center front.

Monkeying around: There is plenty of evidence to show that monkeys have a mischievous sense of humor.

Eye piece

Sew eye piece to head, sitting it on top of muzzle, using back stitch around outside edge.

Ears

Join row-ends of ears and with seam at center back. Sew ears to head halfway down.

Tail

Join row-ends of tail on right side using mattress stitch. Sew tail to body.

Banana

Gather cast-on sts of banana and join row-ends, leaving a gap in the middle. Stuff, pushing stuffing into both ends with tweezers or the tip of scissors. Close gap and sew a running st along seam and pull tight and secure to make bend in banana.

Banana skins and skin linings

With wrong sides together, place a skin and a lining together matching all the edges and whipstitch row-ends together. Do this for 3 skins. Place skins in a row and join row-ends of cast-on sts to form a ring around the banana. Position skins halfway up banana and sew cast-on sts of skin linings and skins to banana all the way around.

Embroidering the features

To make eyes, tie a knot in two lengths of black yarn winding the yarn around 6 times to make each knot (see page 122). Check that the knots are the same size. Tie eyes to head, with 5 knitted sts in between and weave ends into head. Embroider nose in black taking a straight st over 2 sts and for mouth, a curved line in backstitch with a straight st at each end. To begin and fasten off invisibly for the embroidery, tie a knot in end of yarn and take a big st through work, coming up to start embroidery. Allow knot to disappear through knitting and be caught in stuffing. To fasten off, take a few sts back and forth through work, inserting the needle where yarn comes out.

Snakes grow their entire lives. As long as there is food to eat, they just keep getting bigger. Many snakes regularly eat prey that is up to 20 percent of their body size—that's like trying to stuff a whole watermelon in your mouth!—but they've been known to eat prey that is a lot, lot larger. . . . Depending on the size of the meal, a snake may not eat again for several weeks or months.

SNAKES

DID YOU KNOW? Snakes can't hear the snake-charmer's flute; they just feel vibrations and that's why they dance.

What you'll need

Measurement
Each snake measures 23½in (60cm) from head to tail

Materials
Any light worsted weight yarn:
175yd (1¾oz/50g) khaki green (A – main color for first snake)
175yd (1¾oz/50g) mulberry (A – main color for second snake)
175yd (1¾oz/50g) black (B)
175yd (1¾oz/50g) mustard (C)
Scrap of red (D)
Note: amounts are generous but approximate

A pair of size 3 U.S. (3.25mm) needles
Polyester fiberfill
Straight pins
Tweezers for stuffing small parts (optional)

Gauge
26 sts x 34 rows measure 4in (10cm) square over Stockinette st using size 3 U.S. needles before stuffing

Abbreviations
See page 124

How to make a Snake

Head
Beg at neck using the thumb method and A, cast on 30 sts.
P 1 row.
Inc row: K2, (m1, k2) to end (44 sts).
Beg with a p row, work in St st for 21 rows.
Dec row: (K2, k2tog) to end (33 sts).
P 1 row.
Dec row: (K1, k2tog) to end (22 sts).
Beg with a p row, work in St st for 9 rows.
Dec row: K1, (k2tog) to last st, k1 (12 sts).
Bind off p-wise.

Body
Beg at neck using the thumb method and B, cast on 30 sts.
P 1 row.
Begin stripe patt
Join on A and C and work in stripe as follows, carrying yarn loosely up side of work.

Beg with a k row, work in St st for 4 rows, C.
Work in St st for 2 rows, B.
Work in St st for 6 rows, A.
Work in St st for 2 rows, B.
This sets the stripe patt and is repeated for 120 more rows, ending 2 rows into the 10th stripe in A.

Shape tail
Keeping stripe patt correct, work 45 rows, decreasing 1 st at each end of next and every foll 4th row to 6 sts.
P 1 row.
Thread yarn through sts, pull tight and secure.

Tongue (make 2 pieces)
Using the thumb method and D, cast on 18 sts.
Bind off loosely, p-wise.

Eyes (make 2)
Using the thumb method and C, cast on 6 sts.
P 1 row.
Inc row: (Inc) to end (12 sts).
Beg with a p row, work in St st for 3 rows.
Change to B.
Work in St st for 2 rows.
Thread yarn through sts, pull tight and secure.

Eyelids (make 2)
Using the thumb method and A, cast on 10 sts.
Beg with a p row, work in St st for 2 rows, ending on a k row.
Dec row: (P2tog) to end (5 sts).
Thread yarn through rem sts, pull tight and secure.

Snakes have always had a bad reputation. What a shame! They're really shy, retiring creatures who like to keep to themselves.

Assembly

Tongue

Place tongue pieces on top of each other matching all edges. Join two-thirds along the edges. Fan out ends into a Y-shape and stitch in place.

Body and head

Sew head to body by joining both sets of cast-on sts. Join row-ends of head and with seam at center underneath, join bound-off sts of mouth, inserting tongue into this seam. Stuff head. With right sides outside and beginning at tail, join row-ends of body using mattress stitch, stuffing lightly as you go and pushing stuffing into tip of tail with tweezers or tip of scissors.

Eyes

Join row-ends of eyes and gather cast-on sts, pull tight and secure. Press eyes flat, like a button, and sew to head, with seam under the eyelid.

Eyelids

Sew eyelids to head, overlapping the eyes. Sew cast-on sts of lids to eyes.

Hippos are adapted for life in the water, spending up to 16 hours a day swimming, walking, or wallowing in rivers and lakes. This keeps them nice and cool under the hot African sun. At sunset they'll leave their watery home in search of juicy grass to graze on, and will happily eat for up to five hours!

HIPPO

What you'll need

Measurement
Hippo measures 8¾in (22cm)
in height

Materials
Any light worsted weight yarn:
350yd (3½oz/100g) blue gray (A)
Scraps of black for features
*Note: amounts are generous
but approximate*
A pair of size 3 U.S. (3.25mm) needles
Polyester fiberfill
Straight pins

Gauge
26 sts x 34 rows measure 4in
(10cm) square over
Stockinette st using
size 3 U.S. (3.25mm)
needles before stuffing

Abbreviations
See page 124

hippo

How to make Hippo

Body (make 2 pieces)

Beg at lower edge using the thumb method and A, cast on 35 sts.

First and next 4 foll alt rows: P.

Inc row: K10, m1, k15, m1, k10 (37 sts).

Inc row: K11, m1, k15, m1, k11 (39 sts).

Inc row: K12, m1, k15, m1, k12 (41 sts).

Inc row: K13, m1, k15, m1, k13 (43 sts).

Inc row: K14, m1, k15, m1, k14 (45 sts).

Beg with a p row, work in St st for 11 rows.

Dec row: K2tog, k to last 2 sts, k2tog tbl.

Next row: P.

Rep last 2 rows 12 more times (19 sts).

Bind off.

Base

Using the thumb method and A, cast on 20 sts.

First row: P.

Inc row: K1, m1, k to last st, m1, k1.

Rep first 2 rows 5 more times (32 sts).

Beg with a p row, work in St st for 5 rows.

Dec row: K2tog, k to last 2 sts, k2tog tbl.

Next row: P.

Rep last 2 rows 5 more times (20 sts).

Bind off.

Head

Using the thumb method and A, cast on 22 sts.

Place a marker at center of cast-on sts.

P 1 row.

Inc row: K2, (m1, k2) to end (32 sts).

Beg with a p row, work in St st for 3 rows.

Inc row: K2, (m1, k4) to last 2 sts, m1, k2 (40 sts).

Beg with a p row, work in St st for 3 rows.

Inc row: K6, (m1, k1) 10 times, k8, (k1, m1) 10 times, k6 (60 sts).

Beg with a p row, work in St st for 21 rows.

Shape top of head

Dec row: (K4, k2tog) to end (50 sts).

Next and next 3 foll alt rows: P.

Dec row: (K3, k2tog) to end (40 sts).

Dec row: (K2, k2tog) to end (30 sts).

Dec row: (K1, k2tog) to end (20 sts).

Dec row: (K2tog) to end (10 sts).

Thread yarn through rem sts, pull tight and secure.

Snout

Beg at center using the thumb method and A, cast on 24 sts.

Place a marker at center of cast-on sts.

P 1 row.

Inc row: K4, (m1, k1) 6 times, k4, (k1, m1) 6 times, k4 (36 sts).

Beg with a p row, work in St st for 3 rows.

Inc row: K4, (m1, k2) 6 times, k4, (k2, m1) 6 times, k4 (48 sts).

Beg with a p row, work in St st for 11 rows.

Dec row: (K4, k2tog) to end (40 sts).

P 1 row.

Bind off.

Hind legs (make 2)

Note: Follow individual instructions for right and left legs.

Beg at sole using the thumb method and A, cast on 22 sts.

Place a marker at center of cast-on sts.

P 1 row.

Inc row: K1, (m1, k1) to end (43 sts).

Beg with a p row, work in St st for 17 rows.

Dec for right leg: K4, (k2tog) 10 times, k19 (33 sts).

Dec for left leg: K19, (k2tog) 10 times, k4 (33 sts).

Beg with a p row, work in St st for 5 rows.

Bind off 9 sts at beg of next 2 rows (15 sts).

Dec row: (K2tog) twice, k to last 4 sts, k2tog, k2tog tbl.

Dec row: P2tog tbl, p to last 2 sts, p2tog.

Rep last 2 rows once (3 sts).

Bind off.

Forelegs (make 2)

Beg at lower edge using the thumb method and A, cast on 14 sts.

First and next 3 foll alt rows: P.

Inc row: K2, (m1, k2) to end (20 sts).

Inc row: (K1, m1, k8, m1, k1) twice (24 sts).

Inc row: (K1, m1, k10, m1, k1) twice (28 sts).

Inc row: (K1, m1, k12, m1, k1) twice (32 sts).

Beg with a p row, work in St st for 3 rows.

Dec row: (K1, k2tog, k10, k2tog tbl, k1) twice (28 sts).

DID YOU KNOW? A hippopotamus has no sweat glands. They roll around in mud or dunk into water to keep cool.

Next and next foll alt row: P.
Dec row: (K1, k2tog, k8, k2tog tbl, k1)
twice (24 sts).
Dec row: (K1, k2tog, k6, k2tog tbl, k1)
twice (20 sts).
Beg with a p row, work in St st for 11 rows.
Dec row: (K2tog) to end (10 sts).
Bind off p-wise.

Ears (make 2)
Beg at lower edge using the thumb method
and A, cast on 8 sts.
P 1 row.
Inc row: K1, (m1, k1) to end (15 sts).
Beg with a p row, work in St st for 5 rows.
Dec row: (K1, k2tog) to end (10 sts).
Thread yarn through rem sts, pull tight
and secure.

Tail
Using the thumb method and A, cast on
8 sts.
Beg with a p row, work in St st for 9 rows.
Bind off.

Assembly
Body
Place the two halves of body together
matching all edges and join row-ends. Stuff
body leaving neck and lower edge open.

Base
Pin base to lower edge of body and
sew base to body all the way around,
adding more stuffing to base
if needed.

Head
Join row-ends of head and stuff. Bring
marker at cast-on edge and seam together
and whipstitch cast-on sts. Place cast-on sts
of head at center front of neck with seam
underneath and join, adding more stuffing
to neck if needed. Sew back of head to
neck by taking a small horizontal st from
head then a small horizontal st from
neck, alternating all the way around.

Snout
Join row-ends of snout. Bringing row-ends
and marker together join cast-on sts. Stuff
snout and with seam at center, underneath,
pin and sew snout to center of lower half
of head.

Hind legs
Join row-ends of hind legs and bringing
marker and seam together, whipstitch
cast-on sts. Stuff legs, pushing stuffing into
toes. Stand body on flat surface and pin
legs to body. Sew legs to body all the
way around.

Forelegs
Fold cast-on sts of forelegs in half and
whipstitch. Fold bound-off sts in half and
whipstitch. Join row-ends leaving a gap,
stuff and close gap. Sew forelegs to either
side of body, sewing bound-off sts to neck.

Ears
Join row-ends of ears and with seam at
center back, sew ears to head.

Tail
Make a small tassel in A (see page 122)
and anchor it to inside edge of one end
of tail. Gather this end and pull tight and
secure. Join row-ends of tail on right side
using mattress stitch. Sew tail to back
of hippo.

Embroidering the features
To make eyes, tie a knot in two lengths of
black yarn winding the yarn around 6 times
to make each knot (see page 122). Check
that the knots are the same size. Tie eyes
to head on 2nd row above snout with 8
knitted sts in between and weave ends into
head. Embroider nostrils in black taking 2
straight sts close together for each nostril
at sides of snout. For mouth, embroider
a curved line in backstitch with a straight
st at each end. To begin and fasten off
invisibly for embroidery, tie a knot in end
of yarn and take a big st through work,
coming up to start embroidery. Allow the
knot to disappear through knitting and be
caught in stuffing. To fasten off, take a few
sts back and forth through work, inserting
the needle where yarn comes out.

A group of rhinos is called a "crash"—an appropriate term for a large animal that can crash through just about anything in its way. Rhinos may look indestructible, but their skin is actually quite sensitive, especially to sunburn and biting insects. That's why they like to wallow in mud.

RHINO

What you'll need

Measurement
Rhino measures 8¾in (22cm)
in height

Materials
Any light worsted weight yarn:
350yd (3½oz/100g) gray (A)
70yd (¾oz/20g) white (B)
Scrap of black for features
Note: amounts are generous
but approximate
A pair of size 3 U.S. (3.25mm) needles
Polyester fiberfill
Straight pins
Tweezers for stuffing small parts
(optional)

Gauge
26 sts x 34 rows measure 4in (10cm)
square over Stockinette st using size 3
U.S. needles before stuffing

Abbreviations
See page 124

DID YOU KNOW? Rhino horns can grow again. They're made of compressed keratin fibers, just like our fingernails.

rhino

How to make Rhino

Body (make 2 pieces)
Beg at lower edge using the thumb method and A, cast on 35 sts.

First and next 4 foll alt rows: P.
Inc row: K10, m1, k15, m1, k10 (37 sts).
Inc row: K11, m1, k15, m1, k11 (39 sts).
Inc row: K12, m1, k15, m1, k12 (41 sts).
Inc row: K13, m1, k15, m1, k13 (43 sts).
Inc row: K14, m1, k15, m1, k14 (45 sts).
Beg with a p row, work in St st for 11 rows.
Dec row: K2tog, k to last 2 sts, k2tog tbl.
Next row: P.
Rep last 2 rows 12 more times (19 sts).
Bind off.

Base
Using the thumb method and A, cast on 20 sts.

First row: P.
Inc row: K1, m1, k to last st, m1, k1.
Rep first 2 rows 5 more times (32 sts).

Beg with a p row, work in St st for 5 rows.
Dec row: K2tog, k to last 2 sts, k2tog tbl.
Next row: P.
Rep last 2 rows 5 more times (20 sts).
Bind off.

Head
Beg at lower front edge using the thumb method and A, cast on 22 sts.
Place a marker at center of cast-on sts.
P 1 row.

Inc row: K2, (m1, k2) to end (32 sts).
Beg with a p row, work in St st for 3 rows.
Inc row: K2, (m1, k4) to last 2 sts, m1, k2 (40 sts).
Beg with a p row, work in St st for 3 rows.
Inc row: K8, (m1, k1) 5 times, k14, (k1, m1) 5 times, k8 (50 sts).
Beg with a p row, work in St st for 21 rows.
Shape top of head
Dec row: (K3, k2tog) to end (40 sts).
Next and next 2 foll alt rows: P.
Dec row: (K2, k2tog) to end (30 sts).
Dec row: (K1, k2tog) to end (20 sts).
Dec row: (K2tog) to end (10 sts).
Thread yarn through rem sts, pull tight and secure.

Snout
Using the thumb method and A, cast on 40 sts.
Beg with a p row, work in St st for 3 rows.
Dec row: (K8, k2tog twice, k8) twice (36 sts).
Beg with a p row, work in St st for 3 rows.
Dec row: (K7, k2tog twice, k7) twice (32 sts).
Beg with a p row, work in St st for 3 rows.
Dec row: (K6, k2tog twice, k6) twice (28 sts).
Beg with a p row, work in St st for 9 rows.
Garter st 2 rows.
Dec row: (K2, k2tog twice, k2, k2tog twice, k2) twice (20 sts).
P 1 row.
Dec row: (K3, k2tog twice, k3) twice (16 sts).
Dec row: (P2, p2tog twice, p2) twice (12 sts).
Bind off.

Hind legs (make 2)
Using the thumb method and A, cast on 36 sts.
Beg with a p row, work in St st for 21 rows.
P 2 rows.
Dec row: (K2, k2tog) to end (27 sts).
Next and next foll alt row: P.
Dec row: (K1, k2tog) to end (18 sts).
Dec row: (K2tog) to end (9 sts).
Thread yarn through rem sts, pull tight and secure.

Forelegs (make 2)
Beg at shoulder using the thumb method and A, cast on 14 sts.
P 1 row.
Inc row: K1, (m1, k1) (27 sts).
Beg with a p row, work in St st for 25 rows.
P 2 rows.
Dec row: (K1, k2tog) to end (18 sts).

Yes, the horse has been around as long as I have, but I've got horns. Two, actually.

P 1 row.
Dec row: (K2tog) to end (9 sts).
Thread yarn through rem sts, pull tight and secure.

Large horn
Beg at base using the thumb method and B, cast on 16 sts.
Beg with a p row, work in St st for 5 rows.
Dec row: K5, k2tog, k2, k2tog, k5 (14 sts).
Next and next 3 foll alt rows: P.
Dec row: K4, k2tog, k2, k2tog, k4 (12 sts).
Dec row: K3, k2tog, k2, k2tog, k3 (10 sts).
Dec row: K2, k2tog, k2, k2tog, k2 (8 sts).
Dec row: (K2tog) to end (4 sts).
Thread yarn through rem sts, pull tight and secure.

Small horn
Beg at base using the thumb method and B, cast on 12 sts.
Beg with a p row, work in St st for 3 rows.
Dec row: K3, k2tog, k2, k2tog, k3 (10 sts).
Next and next foll alt row: P.
Dec row: K2, k2tog, k2, k2tog, k2 (8 sts).
Dec row: (K2tog) to end (4 sts).
Thread yarn through rem sts, pull tight and secure.

Ears (make 2)
Beg at base using the thumb method and A, cast on 14 sts.
P 1 row.
Inc row: K2, (m1, k2) to end (20 sts).
Beg with a p row, work in St st for 3 rows.
Dec row: K2tog twice, k12, k2tog, k2tog tbl (16 sts).
Beg with a p row, work in St st for 3 rows.
Dec row: K2tog twice, k8, k2tog, k2tog tbl (12 sts).
P 1 row.
Dec row: (K2tog) to end (6 sts).
Thread yarn through rem sts, pull tight and secure.

Tail
Using the thumb method and A, cast on 8 sts.
Beg with a p row, work in St st for 9 rows.
Bind off.

Assembly
Body
Place two halves of the body together matching all edges and join row-ends. Stuff body leaving neck and lower edge open.

Base
Pin base to lower edge of body and sew base to body all the way around, adding more stuffing to base if needed.

Head
Join row-ends of head and stuff. Bring the marker at cast-on edge and seam together and whipstitch cast-on sts. Place cast-on sts of head at center front of neck with seam underneath and join, adding more stuffing to neck if needed. Sew back of head to neck by taking a small horizontal st from head then a small horizontal st from neck, alternating all the way around.

Snout
Join row-ends of snout and with seam at center of underneath, over-sew cast-off sts. Stuff snout and with seam at center of underneath, pin and sew snout to center of lower half of head.

Hind legs
Join row-ends of hind legs and stuff, leaving cast-on sts at top of legs open. Stand body on flat surface and pin legs to body. Sew legs to body all the way around.

Forelegs
Join row-ends of forelegs and stuff. With seam at center of inside edge, whipstitch cast-on sts and sew forelegs to either side of body, sewing cast-on sts to neck.

Ears
Join row-ends of ears with seam at center back and fold cast-on sts of ears in half and whipstitch. Sew ears to head.

Horns
Join row-ends of each horn and stuff, pushing stuffing into tips with tweezers. Sew horns to snout with seams at center back, the small horn behind the large horn.

Tail
Make a small tassel in A (see page 122) and anchor it to inside edge of one end of tail. Gather this end and pull tight and secure. Join row-ends of tail on right side using mattress stitch. Sew tail to back of rhino.

Embroidering the features
To make eyes, tie a knot in two lengths of black yarn winding the yarn around 6 times to make each knot (see page 122). Check that the knots are the same size. Tie eyes to head on 4th row above snout with 7 knitted sts in between and weave ends into head.

Warthogs can weigh as much as 330 pounds. They may not be the most beautiful of creatures, but they have remarkable strength, flexibility, and intelligence! Instead of wasting time digging their own burrows they find abandoned ones that they enter back-end first, ready to burst out at any moment.

WARTHOG

Warthogs run with their tails sticking up in the air!

What you'll need

Measurement
Warthog measures 8½in (22cm) in height

Materials
Any light worsted weight yarn:
350yd (3½oz/100g) rust (A)
70yd (¾oz/20g) white (B)
Scrap of black for features
*Note: amounts are generous
but approximate*
A pair of size 3 U.S. (3.25mm) needles
Polyester fiberfill
Straight pins
Tweezers for stuffing small parts (optional)

Gauge
26 sts x 34 rows measure 4in (10cm) square
over Stockinette st using size 3 U.S. needles
before stuffing

Abbreviations
See page 124

How to make Warthog

Body (make 2 pieces)
Beg at lower edge using the thumb method and A, cast on 35 sts.
First and next 4 foll alt rows: P.
Inc row: K10, m1, k15, m1, k10 (37 sts).
Inc row: K11, m1, k15, m1, k11 (39 sts).
Inc row: K12, m1, k15, m1, k12 (41 sts).
Inc row: K13, m1, k15, m1, k13 (43 sts).
Inc row: K14, m1, k15, m1, k14 (45 sts).
Beg with a p row, work in St st for 11 rows.
Dec row: K2tog, k to last 2 sts, k2tog tbl.
Next row: P.
Rep last 2 rows 12 more times (19 sts).
Bind off.

Base
Using the thumb method and A, cast on 20 sts.
First row: P.
Inc row: K1, m1, k to last st, m1, k1.
Rep first 2 rows 5 more times (32 sts).
Beg with a p row, work in St st for 5 rows.
Dec row: K2tog, k to last 2 sts, k2tog tbl.
Next row: P.
Rep last 2 rows 5 more times (20 sts).
Bind off.

Head
Beg at lower front edge using the thumb method and A, cast on 22 sts.
Place a marker at center of cast-on sts.
P 1 row.
Inc row: K2, (m1, k2) to end (32 sts).
Beg with a p row, work in St st for 3 rows.
Inc row: K2, (m1, k4) to last 2 sts, m1, k2 (40 sts).
Beg with a p row, work in St st for 3 rows.
Inc row: K8, (m1, k1) 5 times, k14, (k1, m1) 5 times, k8 (50 sts).
Beg with a p row, work in St st for 21 rows.
Shape top of head
Dec row: (K3, k2tog) to end (40 sts).
Next and 2 foll alt rows: P.
Dec row: (K2, k2tog) to end (30 sts).
Dec row: (K1, k2tog) to end (20 sts).
Dec row: (K2tog) to end (10 sts).
Thread yarn through rem sts, pull tight and secure.

Snout
Using the thumb method and A, cast on 40 sts.
Beg with a p row, work in St st for 3 rows.
Dec row: (K8, k2tog twice, k8) twice (36 sts).
Beg with a p row, work in St st for 3 rows.
Dec row: (K7, k2tog twice, k7) twice (32 sts).
Beg with a p row, work in St st for 3 rows.
Dec row: (K6, k2tog twice, k6) twice (28 sts).
Beg with a p row, work in St st for 3 rows.
Work ridge to mark edge of snout.

Beg with a p row, work in St st for 2 rows ending on a k row.
Dec row: (K2, k2tog twice, k2, k2tog twice, k2) twice (20 sts).
Next and next foll alt row: P.
Dec row: (K3, k2tog twice, k3) twice (16 sts).
Dec row: (K2, k2tog twice, k2) twice (12 sts).
Bind off, p-wise.

Hind legs (make 2)
Beg at hoof using the thumb method and A, cast on 13 sts.
P 1 row.
Inc row: K1, (m1, k1) to end (25 sts).
Beg with a p row, work in St st for 5 rows.
Garter st 2 rows.
Beg with a k row, work in St st for 4 rows.
Dec row: K1, (k2tog, k1) to end (17 sts).
Beg with a p row, work in St st for 3 rows.
Inc row: (K2, m1) twice, k9, (m1, k2) twice (21 sts).
Next and next 6 foll alt rows: P.
Inc row: K3, m1, k15, m1, k3 (23 sts).
Inc row: K4, m1, k15, m1, k4 (25 sts).
Inc row: K5, m1, k15, m1, k5 (27 sts).
Inc row: K6, m1, k15, m1, k6 (29 sts).
Inc row: K7, m1, k15, m1, k7 (31 sts).
Inc row: K8, m1, k15, m1, k8 (33 sts).
Inc row: K9, m1, k15, m1, k9 (35 sts).
P 1 row.
Bind off.

Forelegs (make 2)
Beg at hoof using the thumb method and A, cast on 8 sts.
P 1 row.
Inc row: K1, (m1, k1) to end (15 sts).
Beg with a p row, work in St st for 5 rows.
Garter st 2 rows.
Beg with a k row, work in St st for 4 rows.
Dec row: (K1, k2tog) to end (10 sts).
Beg with a p row, work in St st for 3 rows.

Inc row: K2, (m1, k2) to end (14 sts).
Next and next 4 foll alt rows: P.
Inc row: K2, m1, k10, m1, k2 (16 sts).
Inc row: K3, m1, k10, m1, k3 (18 sts).
Inc row: K4, m1, k10, m1, k4 (20 sts).
Inc row: K5, m1, k10, m1, k5 (22 sts).
Inc row: K6, m1, k10, m1, k6 (24 sts).
Beg with a p row, work in St st for 5 rows.
Dec row: (K4, k2tog twice, k4) twice
(20 sts).
Next and next foll alt row: P.
Dec row: (k3, k2tog twice, k3) twice
(16 sts).
Dec row: (k2, k2tog twice, k2) twice
(12 sts).
P 1 row.
Bind off.

Tusks (make 2)
Beg at lower edge using the thumb method
and B, cast on 8 sts.
Beg with a p row, work in St st for 7 rows.
Dec row: K1, k2tog, k2, k2tog k1 (6 sts).
Beg with a p row, work in St st for 3 rows.
Dec row: K1, (k2tog) twice, k1 (4 sts).
Thread yarn through rem sts, pull tight
and secure.

Ears (make 4 pieces)
Cast on 10 sts.
Beg with a p row, work in St st for 3 rows.
Dec row: K2, k2tog, k2, k2tog, k2 (8 sts).
Beg with a p row, work in St st for 3 rows.
Dec row: K1, k2tog, k2, k2tog, k1 (6 sts).
Beg with a p row, work in St st for 3 rows.
Dec row: (k2tog) to end (3 sts).
Thread yarn through rem sts, pull tight
and secure.

Warts (make 4)
Note: Two separate balls of A are required.
Using the thumb method and one strand
of A, cast on 12 sts.

Join on second ball of A and treat
the 2 strands as one.
P 1 row.
Dec row: (K2tog) to end (6 sts).
Thread yarn through rem sts, pull tight
and secure.

Tail
Using A, cast on 6 sts.
Work in St st for 3in (8cm).
Bind off.

Assembly
Body
Place the two halves of body together
matching all edges and join row-ends. Stuff
body leaving neck and lower edge open.

Base
Pin base to lower edge of body and sew
base to body all the way around, adding
more stuffing to base if needed.

Head
Join row-ends of head and stuff. Bring
marker at cast-on edge and seam together
and whipstitch cast-on sts. Place cast-on
sts of head at center front of neck with
seam underneath and join, adding more
stuffing to neck if needed. Sew back of
head to neck by taking a small horizontal st
from head then a small horizontal st from
neck, alternating all the way around.

Snout
Join row-ends of snout and with seam at
center at underneath, whipstitch bound-off
sts. Stuff snout and with seam at center of
underneath, pin and sew snout to center
of lower half of head.

Warthog: Seen here reversing into his new home.

DID YOU KNOW? A group of warthogs is called a "sounder."

Hind legs

Join row-ends of hooves and with seam at center, underneath, join cast-on sts. Join row-ends of ankle and stuff hoof and ankle. Join row-ends of leg and stuff. To shape hoof, take a length of black yarn and sew a large st around center of hoof, starting and finishing at center back of garter sts of hoof. Pull tight and knot yarn sewing ends into hoof. Place body on a flat surface and pin legs to body and sew bound-off sts of legs to body all the way around.

Forelegs

Make up as for hind legs with seam at center of inside edge. Shape hooves as for hind legs. Sew forelegs to body at each side, sewing bound-off sts to neck.

Tusks

Join row-ends of tusks and stuff, pushing stuffing in with tweezers or tip of scissors. Gather cast-on sts, pull tight and secure. Sew tusks to either side of snout, as shown in photograph.

Ears

Place the two pieces of ears together matching all edges and join row-ends. Sew ears to head.

Warts

Join row-ends of cast-on sts of warts. Sew outer edge of 2 warts to each side of snout and 2 warts to head.

Tail

Make a small tassel (see page 122) using black yarn and anchor it to inside edge of one end of the tail. Gather this end and pull tight and secure. Join row-ends of tail on right side using mattress stitch. Sew tail to back of warthog.

Embroidering the features

To make eyes, tie a knot in two lengths of black yarn winding the yarn around 6 times to make each knot (see page 122). Check that the knots are the same size. Tie eyes to head on 4th row above snout with 6 clear knitted sts in between and weave ends into head.

Koalas live almost entirely on eucalyptus leaves, grinding them with special teeth in their cheeks. These tough leaves are poisonous to most other animals. Koala bears don't usually drink water as they get enough moisture from the leaves. However, this diet doesn't provide many calories, so koalas conserve energy by resting for as much as 20 hours each day.

KOALA

What you'll need

Measurement
Koala measures 9½in (24cm) in height

Materials
Any light worsted weight yarn:
175yd (1¾oz/50g) white (A)
350yd (3½oz/100g) gray (B)
70yd (¾oz/20g) black (C)
Note: amounts are generous but
approximate
A pair of size 3 U.S. (3.25mm) needles
Polyester fiberfill
Straight pins

Gauge
26 sts x 34 rows measure 4in (10cm)
square over Stockinette st using size
3 U.S. needles before stuffing

Abbreviations
See page 124

DID YOU KNOW? A newborn koala
is only the size of a jelly bean.

How to make Koala

Body (make 1 piece in A and 1 piece in B)

Beg at lower edge using the thumb method and A or B, cast on 29 sts.

First and next 4 foll alt rows: P.
Inc row: K7, m1, k15, m1, k7 (31 sts).
Inc row: K8, m1, k15, m1, k8 (33 sts).
Inc row: K9, m1, k15, m1, k9 (35 sts).
Beg with a p row, work in St st for 29 rows.
Dec row: K2tog, k to last 2 sts, k2tog tbl.
Next row: P.
Rep last 2 rows 5 more times (23 sts).
Bind off.

Base

Using the thumb method and A, cast on 16 sts.
First row: P.
Inc row: K1, m1, k to last st, m1, k1.
Rep first 2 rows 4 more times (26 sts).
Beg with a p row, work in St st for 5 rows.
Dec row: K2tog, k to last 2 sts, k2tog tbl.
Next row: P.
Rep last 2 rows 4 more times (16 sts).
Bind off.

Head

Beg at lower edge using the thumb method and B, cast on 8 sts.
First and next 6 foll alt rows: P.
Inc row: (Inc) to end (16 sts).
Inc row: (K1, inc) to end (24 sts).
Inc row: (K2, inc) to end (32 sts).
Inc row: (K3, inc) to end (40 sts).
Inc row: (K4, inc) to end (48 sts).
Inc row: (K5, inc) to end (56 sts).
Inc row: (K6, inc) to end (64 sts).
Beg with a p row, work in St st for 3 rows.
Inc row: K29, (m1, k2) 4 times, k27 (68 sts).
Next and next 2 foll alt rows: P.
Inc row: K31, (m1, k2) 4 times, k29 (72 sts).
Inc row: K33, (m1, k2) 4 times, k31 (76 sts).
Inc row: K35, (m1, k2) 4 times, k33 (80 sts).

Beg with a p row, work in St st for 7 rows.
Dec row: K33, (k2tog, k2) 4 times, k31 (76 sts).
Beg with a p row, work in St st for 3 rows.
Dec row: K31, (k2tog, k2) 4 times, k29 (72 sts).
Beg with a p row, work in St st for 3 rows.

Shape top of head

Dec row: (K7, k2tog) to end (64 sts).
Next and next 6 foll alt rows: P.
Dec row: (K6, k2tog) to end (56 sts).
Dec row: (K5, k2tog) to end (48 sts).
Dec row: (K4, k2tog) to end (40 sts).
Dec row: (K3, k2tog) to end (32 sts).
Dec row: (K2, k2tog) to end (24 sts).
Dec row: (K1, k2tog) to end (16 sts).
Dec row: (K2tog) to end (8 sts).
Thread yarn through rem sts, pull tight and secure.

Hind legs (make 2)

Beg at toes using the thumb method and B, cast on 24 sts.
First and next foll alt row: P.
Inc row: (K5, m1, k2, m1, k5) twice (28 sts).
Inc row: (K6, m1, k2, m1, k6) twice (32 sts).
Beg with a p row, work in St st for 5 rows.
Inc row: (K7, m1, k2, m1, k7) twice (36 sts).
Beg with a p row, work in St st for 5 rows.

Shape leg

Row 1: K27, turn.
Row 2: S1p, p17, turn.
Row 3: S1k, k to end.

Rows 4–6: Beg with a p row, work in St st for 3 rows.
Rep last 6 rows 3 more times.
Dec row: K5, (k2tog) 4 times, k10, (k2tog) 4 times, k5 (28 sts).
P 1 row.
Bind off.

Arms (make 2)

Beg at paw using the thumb method and B, cast on 16 sts.
First and next foll alt row: P.
Inc row: (K3, m1, k2, m1, k3) twice (20 sts).
Inc row: (K4, m1, k2, m1, k4) twice (24 sts).
Beg with a p row, work in St st for 5 rows.
Inc row: (K5, m1, k2, m1, k5) twice (28 sts).
Beg with a p row, work in St st for 5 rows.
Inc row: (K6, m1, k2, m1, k6) twice (32 sts).
Beg with a p row, work in St st for 5 rows.

Shape arm

Row 1: K24, turn.
Row 2: S1p, p15, turn.
Row 3: S1k, k to end.
Row 4: P.
Rows 5–8: Beg with a k row, work in St st for 4 rows.
Rep last 8 rows once more.
Dec row: K4, (k2tog) 4 times, k8, (k2tog) 4 times, k4 (24 sts).
P 1 row.
Bind off.

Nose

Note: Nose is knitted in garter st.
Beg at lower edge using the thumb method and C, cast on 4 sts.
Inc row: Inc, k2, inc (6 sts).
K 1 row.
Inc row: Inc, k4, inc (8 sts).
Work in garter st for 15 rows.

Dec row: K2tog, k4, k2tog tbl (6 sts).
K 1 row.
Dec row: K2tog, k2, k2tog tbl (4 sts).
Bind off k-wise.

Ears (make 2 outside ear pieces and 2 inside ear pieces)

Special abbreviation: loop-st
Insert RH needle into next st, place first finger of LH behind LH needle and wind yarn around needle and finger twice, then just around needle once. Knit st, pulling 3 loops through. Place these loops on LH needle and knit into the back of them. Pull loops down sharply to secure. Cont to next st.

Outside ear piece
Beg at lower edge using the thumb method and B, cast on 4 sts.
First and next 4 foll alt rows: P.
Inc row: (Inc) to end (8 sts).
Inc row: (K1, inc) to end (12 sts).
Inc row: (K2, inc) to end (16 sts).
Inc row: (K3, inc) to end (20 sts).
Inc row: (K4, inc) to end (24 sts).
P 1 row.
Bind off loosely.

Inside ear piece
Note: Follow instructions for 1 right and 1 left inside ear piece.
Beg at lower edge using the thumb method and B, cast on 4 sts.
First and next 4 foll alt rows: P.
Inc row: (Inc) to end (8 sts).
Inc row: (K1, inc) to end (12 sts).
Inc row: (K2, inc) to end (16 sts).
Inc row: (K3, inc) to end (20 sts).
Inc row: (K4, inc) to end (24 sts).

Right ear
Break off B and change to A.
Next row: (WS facing) p1, yb, (loop-st) 14 times, p1, turn.
Bind off 16 sts k-wise (8 sts).
Re-join B.

P 1 row.
Bind off.
Left ear
Next row: (WS facing) p8, join on A and continue across row and p1, yb, (loop-st) 14 times, p1.
Bind off 16 sts k-wise (8 sts).
Using B, bind off rem sts.

Assembly

Body
Place two halves of body together matching all edges and join row-ends. Stuff body leaving neck and lower edge open.

Base
Pin base to lower edge of body and sew base to body all the way around, adding more stuffing to base if needed.

Head
Gather cast-on sts of head, pull tight and secure. Join row-ends of head leaving gap. Stuff, pushing a ball of stuffing into nose, and close gap. Pin head to body adding more stuffing to neck if needed. Sew head in place by taking a small horizontal st from head and then a small horizontal st from body and alternating all the way around.

Hind legs
Join row-ends of each hind leg and with seam at center of inside edge, join cast-on sts. Stuff and join bound-off sts. Place koala on a flat surface and pin legs to body. Curl legs around body and sew in place.

Arms
Join row-ends of each arm and with seam at center of inside edge, join cast-on sts. Stuff and join bound-off sts. Attach arms to koala sewing shoulders to neck and with paws sloping down.

Nose
Sew outside edge of nose to head.

Embroidering the features
To make eyes, tie a knot in 2 lengths of black yarn winding the yarn around 6 times to make each knot (see page 122). Check that the knots are the same size. Tie eyes to 4th row above top of nose with 7 knitted sts in between. Weave end into head. Work a chain stitch in black around outside edge of nose. On all paws, embroider 3 toes in black taking three straight sts at ends of paws, beginning and fastening off invisibly. To begin and fasten off for the embroidery, tie a knot in end of yarn and take a big st through work, coming up to start embroidery. Allow knot to disappear through knitting and be caught in stuffing. To fasten off, take a few sts back and forth through work, inserting the needle where yarn comes out.

Ears
With wrong sides facing, place a piece of outside ear and inside ear together, matching all edges. Tuck inside the bound-off sts of outside edge and join outside edges. Join row-ends of lower edge and sew both ears to head of koala. Finally, cut loops of ears.

The moose is the largest deer in the world, native to North America, Europe and Asia, where they live in mountain meadows and forests. The largest moose weighed in at 1,800 pounds and was 7½ feet tall. Moose have compact bodies with long, powerful legs, so they are excellent runners.

MOOSE

"Moose" comes from an Algonquin word meaning "twig-eater."

What you'll need

Measurement
Moose measures 8¾in (22cm) in height, excluding antlers

Materials
Any light worsted weight yarn:
350yd (3½oz/100g) brown (A)
88yd (1oz/25g) beige (B)
88yd (1oz/25g) cream (C)
Scrap of black for features
Note: amounts are generous but approximate
A pair of size 3 U.S. (3.25mm) needles
Polyester fiberfill
Straight pins

Gauge
26 sts x 34 rows measure 4in (10cm) square over Stockinette st using size 3 U.S. needles before stuffing

Abbreviations
See page 124

moose

How to make Moose

Body (make 2 pieces)

Beg at lower edge using the thumb method and A, cast on 35 sts.

First and next 4 foll alt rows: P.

Inc row: K10, m1, k15, m1, k10 (37 sts).

Inc row: K11, m1, k15, m1, k11 (39 sts).

Inc row: K12, m1, k15, m1, k12 (41 sts).

Inc row: K13, m1, k15, m1, k13 (43 sts).

Inc row: K14, m1, k15, m1, k14 (45 sts).

Beg with a p row, work in St st for 11 rows.

Dec row: K2tog, k to last 2 sts, k2tog tbl.

Next row: P.

Rep last 2 rows 12 times more (19 sts).

Bind off.

Base

Using the thumb method and A, cast on 20 sts.

First row: P.

Inc row: K1, m1, k to last st, m1, k1.

Rep these 2 rows 5 times more (32 sts).

Beg with a p row, work 5 rows in St st.

Dec row: K2tog, k to last 2 sts, k2tog tbl.

Next row: P.

Rep last 2 rows 5 times more (20 sts).

Bind off.

Head

Beg at lower front edge using the thumb method and A, cast on 22 sts.

Place a marker at center of cast-on sts.

P1 row.

Inc row: K2, (m1, k2) to end (32 sts).

Beg with a p row, work in St st for 3 rows.

Inc row: K2, (m1, k4) to last 2 sts, m1, k2 (40 sts).

Beg with a p row, work in St st for 3 rows.

Inc row: K8, (m1, k1) 5 times, k14, (k1, m1) 5 times, k8 (50 sts).

Beg with a p row, work in St st for 21 rows.

Shape top of head

Dec row: (K3, k2tog) to end (40 sts).

Next and next 2 foll alt rows: P.

Dec row: (K2, k2tog) to end (30 sts).

Dec row: (K1, k2tog) to end (20 sts).

Dec row: (K2tog) to end (10 sts).

Thread yarn through rem sts, pull tight and secure.

Muzzle

Beg at lower edge using the thumb method and A, cast on 18 sts.

Place a marker at center of cast-on sts.

P 1 row.

Inc row: K4, (m1, k1) 3 times, k4, (k1, m1) 3 times, k4 (24 sts).

Beg with a p row, work in St st for 3 rows.

Inc row: K4, (m1, k1) 6 times, k4, (k1, m1) 6 times, k4 (36 sts).

Beg with a p row, work in St st for 9 rows.

Dec row: (K4, k2tog) to end (30 sts).

Beg with a p row, work in St st for 7 rows.

Bind off.

Hind legs (make 2)

Beg at hoof using the thumb method and B cast on 13 sts.

P 1 row.

Inc row: K1, (m1, k1) to end (25 sts).

Beg with a p row, work in St st for 5 rows.

Garter st 2 rows.

Change to A.

Beg with a k row, work in St st for 4 rows.

Dec row: K1, (k2tog, k1) to end (17 sts).

Beg with a p row, work in St st for 3 rows.

Inc row: K1, (m1, k3) to last st, m1, k1.

P 1 row.

Rep last inc row once (31 sts).

Beg with a p row, work in St st for 13 rows.

Dec row: K1, (k2tog, k1) to end (21 sts).

P 1 row.

Bind off.

Forelegs (make 2)

Beg at hoof using the thumb method and A, cast on 8 sts.

P 1 row.

Inc row: K1, (m1, k1) to end (15 sts).

Beg with a p row, work in St st for 5 rows.

Work in garter st for 2 rows.

Change to A.

Beg with a k row, work in St st for 4 rows.

Dec row: (K1, k2tog) to end (10 sts).

Beg with a p row, work in St st for 3 rows.

Inc row: K2, (m1, k2) to end.

P 1 row.

Rep last inc row once (20 sts).

Beg with a p row, work in St st for 15 rows.

Dec row: (K2, k2tog) to end (15 sts).

P 1 row.

Bind off.

Ears (make 2)

Beg at lower edge using the thumb method and A, cast on 10 sts.

P 1 row.

Inc row: K2, (m1, k2) to end (14 sts).

Beg with a p row, work in St st for 3 rows.

Dec row: K2, (k2tog, k2) to end (11 sts).

Beg with a p row, work in St st for 3 rows.

Dec row: (K2tog) twice, k3, (k2tog) twice (7 sts).

Dec row: P1, (p2tog, p1) twice (5 sts).

Thread yarn through rem sts, pull tight and secure.

Antlers (make 2)

Note: Antlers are worked in garter st.

Beg at lower edge using C, cast on 8 sts.

Inc row: Inc, k to last st, inc.

Rep last row once (12 sts).

Bind off 4 sts at beg of next 2 rows (4 sts).

Work in garter st for 2 rows.

Cast on 3 sts at beg of next 2 rows, knitting the 4th st of these rows tbl (10 sts).

Inc row: Inc, k to last st, inc.
Rep last row 5 times more (22 sts).
Bind off 8 sts at beg of next 2 rows (6 sts).
Work in garter st for 2 rows.
Cast on 3 sts at beg of next 2 rows, knitting the 4th st of these rows tbl (12 sts).
Work in garter st for 2 rows.
Bind off 4 sts at beg of next 2 rows (4 sts).
Work in garter st for 2 rows.
Cast on 3 sts at beg of next 2 rows, knitting the 4th st of these rows tbl (10 sts).
Work in garter st for 2 rows.
Bind off 2 sts at beg of next 2 rows (6 sts).
Work in garter st for 4 rows.
Dec row: K2tog, k2, k2tog tbl (4 sts).
K 1 row.
Thread yarn through sts, pull tight and secure.

Tail
Using the thumb method and A, cast on 8 sts. Beg with a p row, work in St st for 15 rows. Bind off.

Assembly
Body
Place two halves of body together matching all edges. Join row-ends and stuff, leaving neck and lower edge open.

Base
Pin base to lower edge of body and sew base to body all the way around, adding more stuffing to base if needed.

Head
Join row-ends of head and stuff. Bring marker at cast-on edge and seam together and overcast cast-on sts. Place cast-on sts of head at center front of neck with seam underneath and join, adding more stuffing to neck if needed. Sew back of head to neck by taking a small horizontal st from head then a small horizontal st from neck, alternating all the way around.

Muzzle
Join row-ends of muzzle. Bringing row-ends and marker together, join cast-on sts. Stuff muzzle and with seam at center underneath, pin and sew muzzle to center of lower half of head.

Hind legs
Join row-ends of hooves and with seam at center underneath, join cast-on sts. Join row-ends of ankle and stuff hoof and ankle. Join row-ends of leg and stuff. To shape hoof, take a length of A and sew a large st around center of hoof, starting and finishing at center back of garter sts of hoof. Pull tight and knot yarn sewing ends into hoof. Place body on a flat surface and pin legs to body. Sew bound-off sts of legs to body all the way around.

Forelegs
Make as for hind legs with seam at center of inside edge. Shape hooves as for hind legs. Sew forelegs to body at each side, sewing bound-off sts to neck.

Ears
Join row-ends of ears and with seam at center of inside edge join lower edge. Fold cast-on sts of ears in half and whipstitch. Sew ears to head pointing in opposite directions.

Antlers
Take a pipe cleaner and fold over ⅜in (1cm) at top. Place pipe cleaner down center of antler with folded end at top. Fold antler in half around pipe cleaner matching all edges and starting from the top, join outside edges. When nearly complete, cut pipe cleaner to size and fold over about ⅜in (1cm) at other end. Sew antlers to head in front of ears.

Tail
Make a small tassel in A (see page 122) and anchor it to inside edge of one end of tail. Gather this end and pull tight and secure. Join row-ends of tail on right side using mattress stitch. Sew tail to back of moose.

Embroidering the features
To make eyes, tie a knot in two lengths of black yarn winding the yarn around 6 times to make each knot (see page 122). Check that the knots are the same size. Tie eyes to head on second row above muzzle with 7 knitted sts between and weave end into head. Embroider nostrils in black taking a vertical chain stitch for each nostril at sides of muzzle with 6 knitted sts between. To begin and fasten off invisibly for embroidery, tie a knot in end of yarn and take a big st through work, coming up to start embroidery. Allow knot to disappear through knitting and be caught in stuffing. To fasten off, take a few sts back and forth through work, inserting the needle where yarn comes out.

Although all penguins are native to the southern hemisphere, they're not only found in cold climates. The Galápagos penguin lives near the equator. Penguins cannot fly, but they can swim up to 25 miles per hour, catching squid, octopus, fish, and krill to eat.

PENGUIN

What you'll need

Measurement
Penguin measures 9½in (24cm) in height

Materials
Any light worsted weight yarn:
175yd (1¾oz/50g) black (A)
175yd (1¾oz/50g) white (B)
70yd (¾oz/20g) yellow (C)
70yd (¾oz/20g) orange (D)
70yd (¾oz/20g) gray (E)
Note: amounts are generous but approximate
A pair of size 3 U.S. (3.25mm) needles
Polyester fiberfill
Straight pins
Tweezers for stuffing small parts (optional)

Gauge
26 sts x 34 rows measure 4in (10cm) square over Stockinette st using size 3 U.S. needles before stuffing

Abbreviations
See page 124

penguin

DID YOU KNOW? The male emperor penguin holds the egg on the top of his feet with his belly hanging over it. He does this for nine weeks before the chick hatches.

How to make Penguin

Back of body and head

Beg at base using the thumb method and A, cast on 5 sts.

P 1 row.

Inc row: (Inc) to end (10 sts).

Beg with a p row, work in St st for 3 rows.

Inc row: (Inc) to end (20 sts).

Beg with a p row, work in St st for 3 rows.

Inc row: (K1, inc) to end (30 sts).

Beg with a p row, work in St st for 3 rows.

Inc row: (K2, inc) to end (40 sts).

P 1 row.

Place markers at beg and end of last row.

Shape tail

Inc row: K17, (inc) twice, k2, (inc) twice, k17 (44 sts).

Next and next 2 foll alt rows: P.

Inc row: K19, (inc) twice, k2, (inc) twice, k19 (48 sts).

Inc row: K21, (inc) twice, k2, (inc) twice, k21 (52 sts).

Inc row: K23, (inc) twice, k2, (inc) twice, k23 (56 sts).

Beg with a p row, work in St st for 13 rows.

Dec row: K25, k2tog, k2, k2tog, k25 (54 sts).

Next and next 8 foll alt rows: P.

Dec row: K24, k2tog, k2, k2tog, k24 (52 sts).

Dec row: K23, k2tog, k2, k2tog, k23 (50 sts).

Dec row: K22, k2tog, k2, k2tog, k22 (48 sts).

Dec row: K21, k2tog, k2, k2tog, k21 (46 sts).

Dec row: K20, k2tog, k2, k2tog, k20 (44 sts).

Dec row: K19, k2tog, k2, k2tog, k19 (42 sts).

Dec row: K18, k2tog, k2, k2tog, k18 (40 sts).

Beg with a p row, work in St st for 9 rows.

Dec row: K6, k2tog, k24, k2tog, k6 (38 sts).

Next and next foll alt row: P.

Dec row: K6, k2tog, k22, k2tog, k6 (36 sts).

Dec row: K6, k2tog, k20, k2tog, k6 (34 sts).

P 1 row.

Place markers at each end of last row.

Dec row: K6, k2tog, k18, k2tog, k6 (32 sts).

P 1 row.

Shape next row: Inc, k5, k2tog, k16, k2tog, k5, inc.

Next and next 2 foll alt rows: P.

Shape next row: Inc, k6, k2tog, k14, k2tog, k6, inc.

Shape next row: (Inc) twice, k6, k2tog, k12, k2tog, k6, (inc) twice (34 sts).

Shape next row: (Inc) twice, k8, k2tog, k10, k2tog, k8, (inc) twice (36 sts).

P 1 row.

Cast on 6 sts at beg of next 2 rows, working the 7th st of these 2 rows, tbl (48 sts).

Work in St st for 2 rows.

Shape next row: Inc, k16, k2tog, k10, k2tog, k16, inc.

Next and next foll alt row: P.

Shape next row: Inc, k17, k2tog, k8, k2tog, k17, inc.

Shape next row: Inc, k18, k2tog, k6, k2tog, k18, inc.

Beg with a p row, work in St st for 11 rows.

Shape top of head

Dec row: (K4, k2tog) to end (40 sts).

Next and next 3 foll alt rows: P.

Dec row: (K3, k2tog) to end (32 sts).

Dec row: (K2, k2tog) to end (24 sts).

Dec row: (K1, k2tog) to end (16 sts).

Dec row: (K2tog) to end (8 sts).

Thread yarn through rem sts, pull tight and secure.

Front of body

Beg at base using the thumb method and A, cast on 4 sts.

P 1 row.

Inc row: (Inc) to end (8 sts).

Beg with a p row, work in St st for 3 rows.

Inc row: (Inc) to end (16 sts).

Beg with a p row, work in St st for 3 rows.

Inc row: (K1, inc) to end (24 sts).

Beg with a p row, work in St st for 3 rows.

Inc row: (K2, inc) to end (32 sts).

Change to B.

Beg with a p row, work in St st for 45 rows.

Dec row: K1, k2tog, k to last 3 sts, k2tog tbl, k1.

Next row: P.

Rep last 2 rows once (28 sts).

Change to C.

Dec row: K1, k2tog, k to last 3 sts, k2tog tbl, k1.
Next row: P.
Rep last 2 rows 3 more times (20 sts).
Dec row: (K2tog) twice, k to last 4 sts, k2tog, k2tog tbl (16 sts).
P 1 row.
Dec row: (K2tog) twice, k to last 4 sts, k2tog, k2tog tbl (12 sts).
Bind off p-wise.

Feet (make 4)
Note: Feet are worked in garter st.
Using the thumb method and E, cast on 9 sts.
Row 1: K.
Row 2: K4 turn.
Row 3: S1k, k to end.
Row 4: Bind off 3 sts at beg of next row (6 sts).
Row 5: K.
Row 6: Cast on 3 sts at beg of next row and k the 4th st of this row tbl (9 sts).
Rep rows 1–6 once.
Next row: K.
Next row: K4, turn.
Next row: S1k, k to end.
Bind off loosely in garter st.

Flippers (make 2)
First piece
Beg at top edge using the thumb method and A, cast on 8 sts.
Beg with a p row, work in St st for 3 rows.
Inc row: K4, m1, k4 (9 sts).
Beg with a p row, work in St st for 3 rows.
Inc row: K3, m1, k3, m1, k3 (11 sts).
Beg with a p row, work in St st for 3 rows.
Inc row: K3, m1, k5, m1, k3 (13 sts).
Beg with a p row, work in St st for 15 rows.
Dec row: K5, k3tog, k5 (11 sts).
Beg with a p row, work in St st for 3 rows.
Dec row: K4, k3tog, k4 (9 sts).
Beg with a p row, work in St st for 3 rows.
Dec row: K3, k3tog, k3 (7 sts).

Beg with a p row, work in St st for 3 rows.
Dec row: K2, k3tog, k2 (5 sts).
P 1 row.
Dec row: K1, k3tog, k1 (3 sts).
Thread yarn through rem sts, pull tight and secure.
Second piece
Beg at top edge using the thumb method and B, cast on 6 sts.
Beg with a p row, work in St st for 3 rows.
Inc row: K3, m1, k3 (7 sts).
Beg with a p row, work in St st for 3 rows.
Inc row: K2, m1, k3, m1, k2 (9 sts).
Beg with a p row, work in St st for 3 rows.
Inc row: K2, m1, k5, m1, k2 (11 sts).
Beg with a p row, work in St st for 13 rows.
Dec row: K4, k3tog, k4 (9 sts).
Beg with a p row, work in St st for 3 rows.
Dec row: K3, k3tog, k3 (7 sts).
Beg with a p row, work in St st for 3 rows.
Dec row: K2, k3tog, k2 (5 sts).
Beg with a p row, work in St st for 3 rows.
Dec row: K1, k3tog, k1 (3 sts).
Thread yarn through rem sts, pull tight and secure.

Beak
Using the thumb method and D, cast on 9 sts.
Beg with a p row, work in St st for 3 rows.
Dec row: K2tog, k to last 2 sts, k2tog tbl.
Next row: P.
Rep last 2 rows twice (3 sts).
Thread yarn through rem sts, pull tight and secure.

Assembly
Body and head
Join row-ends of head on wrong side from sts on a thread to bound-off sts under chin, sewing back and forth 1 st in from edge. With work inside out, pin front to back, matching first set of markers where black

changes to white on front and second set of markers where white changes to yellow on chest. Leaving base open, sew in place sewing back and forth 1 st in from edge. Stuff head then body, pushing a large ball of stuffing into tail. Join row-ends of base.

Feet
Take 2 pieces of feet and place together matching all edges. Whipstitch both pieces together, sewing cast-on and bound-off sts together and sew around toes. Push a small amount of stuffing inside and overcast straight row-ends. Repeat for second foot. Sew feet to lower edge of penguin.

Flippers
With wrong sides of knitting together, place a first and a second piece of flipper together matching all edges. Slip stitch around all edges and repeat for other flipper. Sew flippers to penguin at each side.

Beak
Join row-ends of beak and stuff, pushing stuffing in with tweezers or tip of scissors. Sew cast-on sts of beak to head all the way around.

Embroidering the features
Using gray, embroider 2 rings in chain stitch for eyes. To begin and fasten off invisibly for the embroidery, tie a knot in end of yarn and take a large st through work, coming up to start the embroidery. Allow knot to disappear through knitting and be caught in stuffing. To fasten off, take a few sts back and forth through work, inserting needle where yarn comes out.

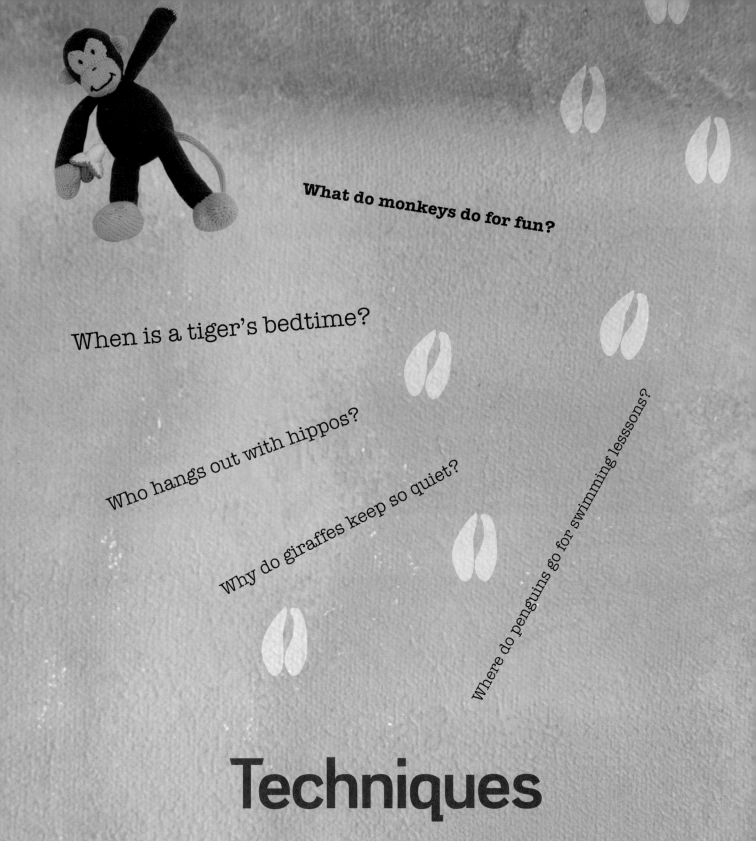

What do monkeys do for fun?

When is a tiger's bedtime?

Who hangs out with hippos?

Why do giraffes keep so quiet?

Where do penguins go for swimming lesssons?

Techniques

Getting started

Buying yarn

All the patterns in this book are worked in double knitting or light worsted weight yarn. There are many yarns on the market, from natural fibers to acrylic blends. Acrylic yarn is a good choice as it washes without shrinking, but always follow the care instructions on the yarn label. Be cautious about using a brushed or mohair type yarn if the toy is intended for a baby or very young child as the fibers can be swallowed.

Gauge

Gauge is not critical when knitting toys if the right yarn and needles are used. All the toys in this book are knitted on size 3 U.S. (3.25mm) knitting needles. This should turn out at approximately 26 stitches and 34 rows over 4in (10cm) square. It is advisable, if using more than one color in the design, to use the same type of yarn as described on the yarn label as some yarns are bulkier and will turn out slightly bigger.

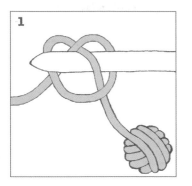

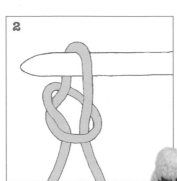

Slip knot

1 Leave a long length of yarn—as a rough guide, allow ⅜in (1cm) for each stitch to be cast on, plus an extra length for sewing up. Wind the yarn from the ball around your left index finger from front to back and then to back again. Slide loop from finger and put loop, from back to front, onto the needle, which is in your right hand.

2 Pull the tail of yarn down to tighten the knot slightly and pull the yarn from the ball to form a loose knot.

Casting on

Thumb method

1 Make a slip knot. Hold the needle in your right hand with your index finger on the slip knot loop to keep it in place.

2 Hold the needle in your right hand and wrap the loose tail end around the left thumb, from front to back. Push the needle point through the thumb loop from front to back. Wind the ball end of yarn around the needle from left to right.

3 Pull the loop through the thumb loop, then remove your thumb. Gently pull the new loop tight using the tail yarn. Repeat until the desired number of stitches are on the needle.

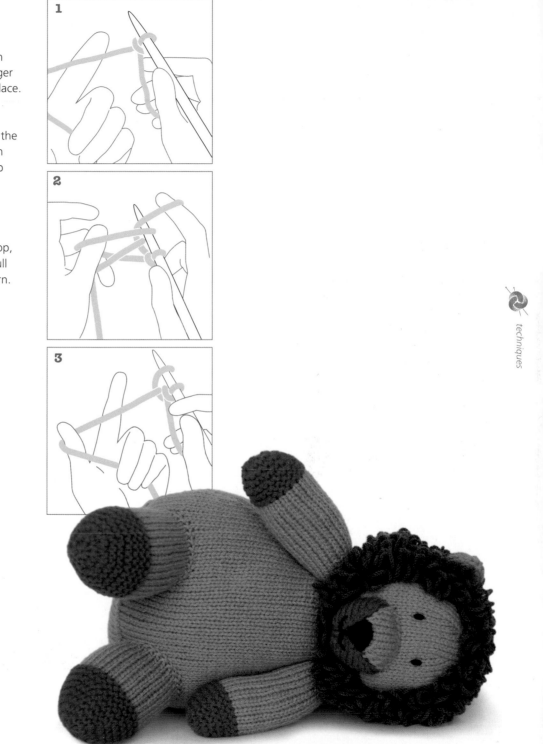

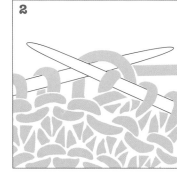

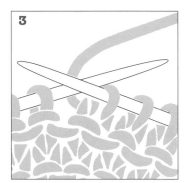

Knit stitch

1 Hold the needle with the cast-on stitches in your left hand. Place the tip of the empty right-hand needle into the first stitch. Wrap the yarn around as for casting on.

2 Pull the yarn through to create a new loop.

3 Slip the new stitch onto the right-hand needle. Continue in the same way for each stitch on the left-hand needle. To start a new row, turn your work to swap the needles and repeat instructions.

Purl stitch

1 Hold the yarn at the front of the work as shown.

2 Place the right-hand needle into the first stitch from front to back. Wrap the yarn counter-clockwise around the right-hand needle as shown.

3 Bring the needle back through the stitch and pull through.

Types of stitches

Garter stitch (A)
Knit every row.

Stockinette stitch (B)
Knit on the right side and purl on the wrong side.

Seed stitch (C)

1 Work Seed stitch (with an odd number of stitches on the needle). With the yarn at the back of the work, knit the first stitch in the normal way.

2 Purl the next stitch, but before you do so, bring the yarn through the 2 needles to the front of your work.

3 With the yarn now at the front, purl the stitch.

4 Next you need to knit a stitch, so take the yarn back between the needles and knit a stitch. Continue to k1, (p1, k1) to the end of the row. This row is repeated.

The patterns in this book only use an odd number of stitches.

Increasing

To increase the number of stitches, there are two methods used in this book: inc and m1.

Inc – Knit twice into the next stitch. To do this on a knit row, simply knit into the next stitch but do not slip it off. Take the point of the right-hand needle around and knit again into the back of the stitch before removing the loop from the left-hand needle.

To do this on a purl row, purl first into the back of the stitch but do not slip it off. Purl again into the front of the stitch before removing the loop from the left-hand needle. You have now made two stitches out of one.

M1 – Make a stitch by picking up the horizontal loop between the needles and placing it on to the left-hand needle. Now knit into the back of it to twist it, or purl into the back of it on a purl row.

Decreasing

To decrease a stitch, simply knit two stitches together to make one out of the two stitches or, if the instructions say k3tog, then knit three stitches together to make one out of the three stitches. To keep your stitches neat, this is done as follows:

At the beginning of a knit row and throughout the row, k2tog by knitting two stitches together through the front of the loops.

At the end of a knit row, if these are the very last two stitches in the row, then knit together through back of loops.

At the beginning of a purl row, if these are the very first stitches in the row, then purl together through back of loops. Purl two together along the rest of the row through the front of the loops.

Intarsia

This technique is used when knitting blocks of color. Use a separate ball for each block, remembering to twist the old and new yarns at the back when changing colors to avoid holes (**diagram below**). Then weave in the ends at the back with a tapestry needle when finished.

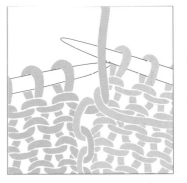

techniques

Peekaboo! Can you see me? I can see you!

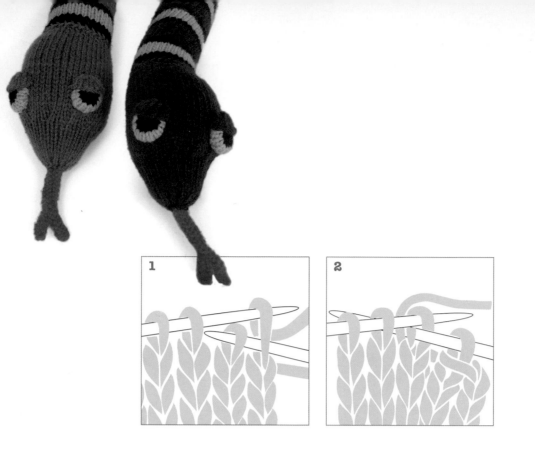

Binding off

1 Knit two stitches on to the right-hand needle, then slip the first stitch over the second and let it drop off the needle. One stitch is remaining.

2 Knit another stitch so you have two stitches on the right-hand needle again.

3 Repeat process until only one stitch is left on the left-hand needle. Break yarn and thread it through remaining stitch.

Koala is inconsolable. We've nearly reached the end.

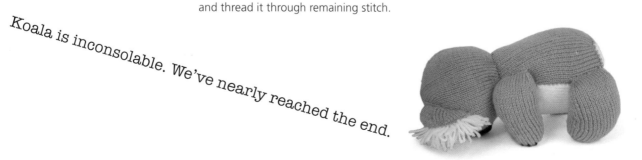

Assembly

The animals in this book are put together using simple sewing techniques.

Mattress stitch

Place the pieces to be joined on a flat surface. Lay them side by side, with right sides towards you. Thread a needle with matching yarn and sew the pieces together with small, straight stitches, back and forth. The stitches form a ladder between the two pieces of fabric, creating a flat, secure seam (diagram right).

Overcasting

With the right sides of the pieces facing each other, insert your needle from back to front through the strands at the edges of the pieces between the knots.

Slip stitch

When attaching a separate piece to the body of your toy, pick up the horizontal bar in the center of a stitch from the body, then the horizontal bar one stitch in from the edge of the piece to be attached. Draw the yarn through.

Whipstitch

Pieces can also be joined by whipstitching on the wrong side and turning the piece right side out. For smaller pieces or pieces that cannot be turned (such as the elephant's tusks or the animals' bases), whipstitch on the right side.

Join row ends

Join row ends on all the animals by sewing back and forth one stitch in from the edge.

Wiser animals know the fun has just begun.

Making tassels

1 Take a piece of stiff cardboard, approximately 3in (8cm) wide, and wrap yarn around it several times. Secure this bundle with a separate length of yarn threaded through at one end, leaving long ends, then cut the bundle at the opposite edge.

2 Keeping the bundle folded in half, wind a separate length of yarn a few times around the whole bundle, including the long ends of the tie, approx. ¾in (2cm) below the fold, to form the head of the tassel. Tie the two ends of this length of yarn together tightly. Trim all the ends of yarn at the base of the tassel to give a tidy finish. If you want a more bushy tassel, unroll and separate the strands of yarn.

Embroidery

To begin embroidery invisibly, tie a knot in the end of the yarn. Take a large stitch through the work, coming up to begin embroidery. Allow the knot to disappear through the knitting and be caught in the stuffing. To fasten off invisibly, sew a few stitches back and forth through the work, inserting the needle where the yarn comes out.

Long stitches
Embroider nostrils, crocodile's teeth, and some mouths by sewing long stitches.

Chain stitch
Embroider crocodile's mouth and panda and penguin's eyes in chain stitch. Bring the needle up and reinsert where it last emerged. Pull the yarn through to form a small loop and bring the point of the needle out at the end of the loop. Keep the yarn under the needle point and then pull the yarn through. Continue in this way to make a chain of stitches.

Backstitch
Embroider monkey and hippo's mouth in backstitch. Bring the needle out at the beginning of the stitch line, take a straight stitch and bring the needle out slightly further along the stitch line. Insert the needle at the end of the first stitch and bring it out still further along the stitch line. Continue in the same way to create a line of joined stitches.

Eyes
1 Make a loose single slip knot and then wind the yarn around five more times, making a total of six times. (The diagram below shows the yarn being wound three more times.) Pull the knot tight.

2 You now have an oval-shaped eye. Make 2 and check that the knots are the same size. Tie eyes to head in position as stated in the instructions. Weave ends into head.

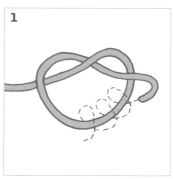

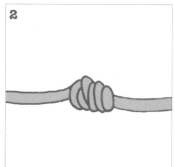

Stuffing and care

Spend a little time stuffing your toy evenly. Polyester fiberfill is ideal and plenty should be used, but not so much that it stretches the knitting and the stuffing can be seen through the stitches. Fill out any base keeping it flat; tweezers are useful for small parts.

Washable filling is recommended for all the stuffed toys so that you can handwash them in a non-biological detergent. Do not spin or tumble dry, but gently squeeze the excess water out, arrange the animal into its original shape and leave to dry.

Abbreviations

alt	alternate
beg	beginning
cm	centimeters
cont	continue
dec	decrease
foll	following
Garter st	Garter stitch: knit every row
g	grams
inc	increase
k	knit
k2tog	knit two stitches together: if these are the very last in the row, then work together through back loop(s)
k3tog	knit three stitches together
k-wise	knitwise
LH	left hand
m1	make one stitch: pick up horizontal loop between the needles and work into the back of it
mm	millimeters
patt	pattern
p	purl
p2tog	purl two stitches together: if these stitches are the very first in the row, then work together through back loop(s)
p3tog	purl three stitches together
p-wise	purlwise
rem	remaining
rep	repeat
RH	right hand
RS	right side
s1k	slip one stitch knitwise
s1p	slip one stitch purlwise
st(s)	stitch(es)
St st	Stockinette stitch: knit on the right side, purl on the wrong side
tbl	through back loop(s)
tog	together
WS	wrong side
yb	yarn back
( )	repeat instructions between parentheses as many times as instructed

Resources

Yarn substitution chart

Types of yarn in category	Knit gauge range (in Stockinette stitch to 4 inches)	Recommended needle sizes (U.S./metric sizes)
0 LACE — Fingering, 10-count crochet thread	33–40 sts	000–1/1.5–2.25mm
1 SUPER FINE — Sock, fingering, baby	27–32 sts	1–3/2.25–3.25mm
2 FINE — Sport, baby	23–26 sts	3–5/3.25–3.75mm
3 LIGHT — DK, light worsted	21–24 sts	5–7/3.75–4.5mm
4 MEDIUM — Worsted, afghan, aran	16–20 sts	7–9/4.5–5.5mm
5 BULKY — Chunky, craft, rug	12–15 sts	9–11/5.5–8mm
6 SUPER BULKY — Bulky, roving	6–11 sts	11 and larger/8mm and larger

Adapted from the Standard Yarn Weight System of the Craft Yarn Council of America.

Online resources

Craft
www.craftzine.com

Craft Yarn Council of America
www.craftyarncouncil.com

Knitter's Review
www.knittersreview.com

Knitting Daily
www.knittingdaily.com

KnittingHelp
www.knittinghelp.com

Knitting on the Net
www.knittingonthenet.com

The Daily Knitter
www.dailyknitter.com

The Knitting Site
www.theknittingsite.com

Ravelry
www.ravelry.com

Materials and supplies

You can find the type of yarn used in this book—light worsted weight, also known as DK, which is designated with a "3" in the Yarn Weights chart below—along with the other knitting supplies noted in the materials lists for each project at your local yarn or crafts retailer.

About the author

Sarah Keen was born and brought up in Wales in the UK. She discovered a love of knitting at a very early age: her mother taught her to knit when she was just four years old and by the age of nine she was making jackets and jumpers.

Sarah now works as a freelance pattern designer and finds calculating rows and stitches challenging but fascinating. She is experienced in designing knitted toys for children, having made several for her nephews and nieces. She also enjoys writing patterns for charity and publishes them at home. Sarah is passionate about knitting, finding it relaxing and therapeutic—and very addictive! This is her first book.

Your heyday is not over yet, Hippo.

Index

index